D0994499

FREEDOM
REGAINED

Also by Julian Baggini

The Virtues of the Table: How to Eat and Think

The Ego Trick

Should You Judge this Book by Its Cover?: 100 Fresh Takes on Familiar Sayings and Quotations

Do They Think You're Stupid?: 100 Ways of Spotting Spin & Nonsense from the Media, Pundits & Politicians

Welcome to Everytown: A Journey into the English Mind

The Pig That Wants to be Eaten: And 99 Other Thought Experiments

What's It All About? – Philosophy and the Meaning of Life

By Julian Baggini and Jeremy Stangroom

Do You Think What You Think You Think?

FREEDOM REGAINED

The Possibility of Free Will

Julian Baggini

GRANTA

Granta Publications, 12 Addison Avenue, London W11 4QR

First published in Great Britain by Granta Books, 2015

Copyright © Julian Baggini 2015

Julian Baggini has asserted his moral right under the Copyright, Designs
and Patents Act, 1988, to be identified as the author of this work.

All rights reserved. This book is copyright material
and must not be copied, reproduced, transferred, distributed,
leased, licensed or publicly performed or used in any way except as
specifically permitted in writing by the publisher, as allowed under
the terms and conditions under which it was purchased or as
strictly permitted by applicable copyright law. Any
unauthorized distribution or use of this text may be a
direct infringement of the author's and publisher's
rights, and those responsible may be
liable in law accordingly.

A CIP catalogue record for this book
is available from the British Library.

123·5

1 3 5 7 9 10 8 6 4 2

ISBN 978 1 84708 717 5
eISBN 978 1 84708 716 4

Printed and bound by CPI Group (UK) Ltd, Croydon, CR0 4YY

MIX
Paper from
responsible sources
FSC
www.fsc.org   FSC® C020471

I own that this dispute has been so much canvassed on all hands, and has led philosophers into such a labyrinth of obscure sophistry, that it is no wonder, if a sensible reader indulge his ease so far as to turn a deaf ear to the proposal of such a question, from which he can expect neither instruction or entertainment.

David Hume, *An Enquiry Concerning Human Understanding* (1748)

Come then come (I say), prove that this dogma of yours about a human vanity and a lie is true.

Martin Luther, *The Enslaved Will* (1525)

Contents

Introduction

[handwritten annotations: "Modality", "Possibility + necessity", "choice", "Forks"]

In the shadow of every life led are all our potential lives not led. Innumerable choices mark the forks in the road, after which there is no turning back: leave school at sixteen or apply for university; stay with a long-term partner or go solo; become a parent or remain childless; accept a job offer or stick with the devil you know; take a train or bus when, unbeknown to you, one of them will end the day a mangled wreck. Right now, you could have chosen to do many things other than sit down to read these words, and if you don't read something interesting pretty soon you may well pick up a different book, go for a walk or switch on the television.

[handwritten annotations: "habit", "repulsion"]

We make countless choices every day, big and small. Even if you are a creature of habit, you are not compelled always to repeat yourself. You may well start each morning with a strong coffee, but at any point you might decide to have a tea instead. You can't do just anything, of course. You can't decide to repeal the Geneva Convention, or jump to the moon. But even excluding the incredibly difficult and the physically impossible, there is always a range of actions that you could choose to do. Within certain limits, you are free to do what you want.

This would appear to be an obvious, even banal, fact about

1

human nature: simple common sense. Yet ever since human beings first started to philosophise, some have denied it. Once science started to mature, more and more rejected free will as an illusion. Read the greatest scientists of the last few hundred years and you'd be excused for thinking that science has disproved free will. Charles Darwin said that 'Everything in nature is the result of fixed laws', and since humans are part of nature, that would seem to mean our actions are also the consequences of the laws of nature, not individual will.[1] 'Everything is determined, the beginning as well as the end, by forces over which we have no control', said Albert Einstein in 1929, even more starkly. 'Human beings, vegetables, or cosmic dust, we all dance to a mysterious tune, intoned in the distance by an invisible piper.'[2] Twenty years later, nothing had changed his mind. 'In human freedom in the philosophical sense I am definitely a disbeliever.'[3]

More recently, Stephen Hawking wrote: 'The initial configuration of the universe may have been chosen by God, or it may itself have been determined by the laws of science. In either case, it would seem that everything in the universe would then be determined by evolution according to the laws of science, so it is difficult to see how we can be masters of our fate.'[4] And perhaps most notoriously of all, Richard Dawkins describes human beings as 'survival machines – robot vehicles blindly programmed to preserve the selfish molecules known as genes'.[5]

In recent years, views like these have become increasingly mainstream. Work in neuroscience has put wind into the sails of those who would deny free will. The springs of our actions do not appear to be our conscious thoughts, desires and intentions but unconscious processes in the brain, ones which often set actions in process before we are even aware of anything. As neuroscientist Sam Harris, one of the most strident recent deniers of free will, sums it up: 'The popular conception of free will seems to rest on two assumptions: (1)

that each of us could have done differently than we did in the past, and (2) that we are the conscious source of most of our thoughts and actions in the present.'[6] Since neither of these assumptions appears to stand up to scientific scrutiny, the game would seem to be over for free will – or at least, the 'popular conception' of it.

'Free will is an illusion' has become such a common claim that it is often accompanied by a knowing 'of course'. Proponents of this view concede that the illusion of freedom is so powerful that denying it usually makes little or no difference to how we act in daily life. Everyone *feels* as though she has free will, they say, even if she knows on reflection that she does not. But this new orthodoxy does not leave the world exactly as it is. Most importantly, it challenges our notions of responsibility. If we accept that all our actions are the inevitable result of causes over which we have no control, then we cannot in good faith continue to hold people morally responsible for their actions. If free will goes, it seems blame and responsibility must go too, and with them the foundations of law and morality. Whenever there is a murder, for example, there is almost always a defence that the killer was himself the victim of forces beyond his control. After James Huberty shot and killed twenty-one people in San Diego in 1984, for example, it was claimed that his rage was the result of monosodium glutamate in McDonald's food and poisoning by lead and cadmium in fumes inhaled while working as a welder.

So is the game really up for free will? I and many other, greater minds don't think so. But at the same time, it is true that the common sense notion of free will is not fit for purpose. It rests on a naive and simplistic assumption that we can rise above our biology and our history to make choices in a condition of unconstrained freedom. The challenges to free will need to be met not by rejecting them wholesale, but by thinking more carefully about what it truly means to be free, rather than what we simply assume it to mean.

3

Free will is an issue of pressing social and political importance. On the one hand, there are those who believe that people are too quick to blame society, their genes, their upbringing or their brain, rather than take responsibility for their actions. As the then British Prime Minister John Major said in 1993, 'Society needs to condemn a little more and understand a little less.'[7] This drives public policies that reduce welfare dependence and state support, and promotes criminal justice policies that replace 'bleeding heart' compassion with more punitive measures. Yet at the same time, other trends stress the ways in which our fates are fixed by a conspiracy of nature and nurture. As a major government report put it in 2011, 'The evidence is clear that children's experiences in their early years strongly influence their outcomes in later life, across a range of areas from health and social behaviour to their employment and educational attainment. The most recent neuroscientific evidence highlights the particular importance of the first three years of a child's life.'[8]

Many governments have also embraced 'nudge' theory, which focuses on the ways in which institutions and processes can be designed to make people do the right thing by tapping into unconscious reactions rather than conscious thoughts and deliberations. This involves numerous small-scale manipulations, which bypass conscious control. For example, telling people that 'nine out of ten people pay their tax on time' makes them more likely to pay on time themselves simply because 'human beings are strongly influenced by what those around them are doing', not because they consciously choose to change their behaviour on the basis of this information.[9]

All this has left us floundering. On the one hand, there is a recognition that we need to encourage a sense of responsibility so that people exercise their freedom. On the other, there is a steady trickle of information suggesting that we are hapless slaves to our genes, our childhood and our environment, and that free will is just a fantasy. We are being pulled in opposing directions, resulting in muddled thinking and contradictory policies.

Fortunately, I think we have at our disposal all the tools we need to rehabilitate a reformed free will.

Free will is one of the most discussed, debated and written-about issues in the history of philosophy. The good news is that that means all the significant landmarks have been discovered, described and analysed in great detail. The bad news is that the maps that plot them are the messy result of the debate's tortuous history and are useful only to academics negotiating their specialised domains. My aim is not so much to claim new discoveries but to redraw the map to highlight the landmarks and pathways that are most helpful for those seeking the way today.

The path I've plotted is divided into five stages. I start with a brief and selective history of the challenges to free will in western philosophy to establish the core perennial issues. This provides the necessary theoretical background for an examination of the major threats to free will that contemporary science is said to pose. I then go back to basics and present a view of what freedom means that starts with human experience, rather than the standard definitions that have come to fill textbooks. Next, I consider cases where free will is compromised, to show how it is not a question of free will, yes or no, but what degrees of freedom we really have. Finally, I bring the arguments together with a positive account of the kind of free will worth wanting.

Thought experiments can often be very useful when making philosophical arguments, and I use some in this book. But I have increasingly come to believe that it is foolish to rely on them when there are real-world examples that are more illuminating. In the case of free will, we have several living, breathing characters that we can look at when considering the limits of and threats to freedom. The four I will focus on are the artist and the dissident as paradigms of freedom, and the addict and the psychopath as exemplars of how freedom can be diminished.

The philosopher Saul Smilansky spoke for many when he told me that: 'In the free will context a lot is at stake; it's a very big deal. Notions like punishment and human self-respect, justification for very important social practices and human interaction, the way we see ourselves and the way we see people that we appreciate or respect.' A lot is indeed at stake, which is why we must not confine ourselves to received wisdom about free will. Free will is neither what it is usually thought to be nor what many want it to be. But what I hope to show is that it simply could never be what it is usually assumed to be, and that no one should want what turns out to be impossible and incoherent. The kind of free will we can have, however, is not only worth wanting but worth striving to achieve.

PART ONE

Freedom Under Threat

1

The Demon

To understand what free will is and why it is under threat, we are going to need to look beyond merely theoretical debates and into the real world. But before we do that, we have to understand the armchair philosophical arguments that have brought the debate to where it is now. There is no better starting point for this than two hundred years ago, when the French mathematician Pierre-Simon Laplace asked what would happen if a vast intellect were to know every law of nature and everything about the state of every object in the universe. The answer would seem to be obvious: like God, it would know all that is, all that had been and all that is to come.

'We may regard the present state of the universe as the effect of its past and the cause of its future,' wrote Laplace.

causality.

An intellect which at a certain moment would know all forces that set nature in motion, and all positions of all items of which nature is composed, if this intellect were also vast enough to submit these data to analysis, it would embrace in a single formula the movements of the greatest bodies of the universe and those of the tiniest atom; for such an intellect nothing would be uncertain and the future just like the past would be present before its eyes.[1]

uncertainly

That intellect has become known as known as Laplace's Demon. Ever since Laplace formulated this hypothesis, philosophers have been haunted by what appears to follow from it. This can be captured in a chain of reasoning that is easy to grasp, disturbing in its consequences but seemingly unavoidable: if everything that happens in the physical universe is the result of prior physical causes and effects, then ultimately everything I do must also be the result of prior physical causes and effects. Everything I say and do is caused by events in my brain, which are themselves caused by other events in my past. Free will has disappeared. Like the weather, what I do may be somewhat unpredictable and sometimes appear fickle, but behind it all is simply the motion of matter, the playing out of the laws of physics.

The key implication of Laplace's thought experiment for free will is easily misunderstood. Many people assume that the most important element in it is the predictability of the future. Free will is challenged because if you can predict with one hundred per cent certainty what will happen, there is no role for freedom to make a difference.

Predictability, however, is not the threat to free will that many take it to be. We can see this in the argument that God's omniscience undermines free will. If God knows everything that has been, is and will be, then he knows everything that you will do. But that would seem to suggest that the future is set, and so you can do nothing to change it. And if you can do nothing to change the future, you have no free will.

This inference seems to me to be wrong. God may simply be able to look ahead and see what you will freely choose to do. Why is that fundamentally different from being able to look back into the past and see what you have already freely chosen to do? God's omniscience merely requires him to be able to jump around in time and so need in no way entail that the future is fixed. Augustine summed this up neatly back in the fourth century: 'Although God foreknows what we are going to will in the future, it does not follow that we do not will by the will. Your blameworthy will ... does not cease to be a will simply because God foreknows that you are going to have it.'[2]

The obvious objection to this is that if God knows what you will do tomorrow, then tomorrow must in some way already be fixed, and that is what undermines free will. But I think this plays on an ambiguity in what 'fixed' means here. If we assume that there is only one past, one present and one future, then once anything is done, history is fixed. We do not believe that therefore nothing in the past was done freely, as we believe that things might have happened differently. The only difference between us and God is that he is able to fast-forward and see what will happen as well as rewind to see what has happened. Of course, there is only one tape to fast-forward, so it might look as though the future is 'fixed'. But just as rewinding allows us to see what people freely chose, even though there is only one tape and one thing they did choose, so fast-forwarding can allow us to see what they will choose, even though there can only ever be one thing they will choose.

In short, there are always many things that could happen but only one that does. To be able to see the future is simply to see the one course of events that transpires. That is no more a reason to believe free will makes no difference to the future as to believe it made no difference to the past.

Although I'm confident this argument is sound, it doesn't matter much for those of us who don't believe in an all-knowing God anyway. (Those who do might also reflect that most supposedly divinely inspired texts seem to assume we do make at least some free choices, so there must be something wrong in the idea that God's existence makes them impossible.) What matters more than predictability for naturalists – those of us who believe that the natural world is all there is and no supernatural forces exist – is whether or not the laws of nature make future events *inevitable*. On this point, naturalists have a free will bogeyman as phoney as the theists' all-knowing God, one that goes by the name of determinism.

Determinism is essentially the thesis that Laplace's demon is a theoretical possibility. We may not know enough ever to predict the future with any great certainty, but the universe is essentially a kind of machine operating according to inviolable laws. And that means everything that happens must happen as a result of the playing out of these laws. To use a somewhat outdated image, atoms bounce off each other, bind to each other, repel and attract each other, and everything we see, from grass growing to composers writing music, is at bottom the inevitable consequence of matter reacting to matter. Similarly, your thoughts and actions are produced by a brain which is just a complicated biological machine, which, like all such mechanisms, from broccoli to fruit flies, requires no free will to make it work.

The contemporary American philosopher Peter van Inwagen has summed up the challenge of determinism to free will in his version of something called the Consequence Argument. 'If determinism is true, then our acts are the consequence of laws of nature and events in the remote past,' he argues. Since 'it's not up to us what went on before we were born, and neither is it up to us what the laws of nature are', it would therefore follow that 'the consequences of these things (including our present acts) are not up to us'.[3] And it just seems obvious that we cannot be responsible for what is not up to us.

Neuroscientist David Eagleman explained to me why he, like many others, sees determinism as lying at the heart of the free will problem. 'If you're looking at the brain, we always study it as a deterministic system: where this goes off, that trips off that neurotransmitter, that causes this to be polarised, and everything happens lock-step from everything else. The heart of the issue is, given that system, it seems hard to figure out how to slip anything else into there.'

Some have sought to save free will by denying Laplacian determinism. Chaos theory appears to offer a scientific way of doing this.
Chaos theory says that complete predictability in physical systems is
in practice impossible because even very tiny changes in initial conditions can lead to very different final outcomes. This is most
famously illustrated by the 'butterfly effect', which suggests that the
tiny disturbances in the air caused by the flapping of an insect's wings
might make the difference between a hurricane blowing on the other
side of the world or not.

Before this became an established scientific fact, the science fiction writer Ray Bradbury had already described the basic idea in his
short story 'A Sound of Thunder', in which a time traveller hunts a
Tyrannosaurus rex.[4] On this safari he has to stay on levitating platforms
and he is only allowed to kill a dinosaur that was going to die at that
precise moment anyway. The time-travel company considers it too
risky to kill even the smallest animal that might otherwise have lived.
'For want of ten mice, a fox dies,' explains the guide. 'For want of ten
foxes a lion starves.' And then one day a caveman starves because 'you,
friend, have stepped on all the tigers in that region. By stepping on
one single mouse.' And that caveman could have been the father of a
'race, a people, an entire history of life'. He warns, 'The stomp of your
foot, on one mouse, could start an earthquake, the effects of which
could shake our earth and destinies down through Time, to their very
foundations.' Yet the time traveller is not careful enough, and one butterfly stuck to the bottom of his boot alters the present he returns to.

Chaos theory may or may not be the end of the hope that human
beings can ever reliably predict the future on the basis of the laws of
physics. But it does not slay Laplace's Demon, since it does not deny
that from the very same starting conditions, only one future would
follow. Chaos theory simply alerts us to the very big differences small
variations can make. This, however, is completely compatible with
Laplacian determinism.

The real challenge to determinism comes from quantum physics. The key feature of quantum theory is that it makes certain laws of nature probabilistic rather than deterministic. From a given set of starting conditions, it is not inevitable what will happen next. In quantum physics you cannot tell, for example, whether a radioactive particle will decay or not in the next ten minutes; you can only assign a probability to its doing so. If quantum theory has got this basic claim right, then Laplace's Demon loses his power. He could not predict the future because not everything that happens according to physical laws *inevitably* happens. Einstein may not have believed it, but God plays dice, so to speak.

But it seems clear to me that the predictability or inevitability of the future is not the real threat to free will that Laplace's thought experiment raises. Take away inevitability from the materialist world view, and you are still left with everything happening as a consequence of matter reacting to matter. The important point is not that everything happens in a way that is absolutely determined. What matters is *matter*: everything is simply the result of physical events behaving solely according to natural laws, deterministic or not.

The problem therefore is not determinism but what is often called the causal closure of the physical domain. That is, every physical event has a physical cause, and neither quantum physics nor chaos theory changes that. A neuron fires because of another neuron, not because some soul-like ghost in the head tells it to. If you zoom down to the most fundamental levels of physical reality, to atoms and beyond, the behaviour of every particle will be explained by its own nature, the nature of those around it and the laws of physics that govern them. Whether or not this makes every event predictable is beside the point. Whether the laws of physics are ultimately deterministic or whether probability has a role, the only causes of neurons firing are physical causes. And that's what leads people to worry about free will.

So the root of scientific scepticism about free will is not determinism but *materialism* – the view that everything is constructed from physical matter. 'The kind of threat to our free will might be called a reductionist threat,' is how philosopher Manuel Vargas puts it. 'It is a threat that seems more rooted in our being built up out of smaller "material" things, than it is a fear about determinism, per se.'[5]

In particular, the worry is that what is really driving us is not desire, belief and thought but small physical processes, atoms colliding. Thoughts, beliefs, desires and feelings are just 'epiphenomena', by-products of neural processes that are the real drivers of action. The man who coined the term 'epiphenomenalism' in 1874, T. H. Huxley, compared the belief that conscious thought drives our behaviour with the belief that the whistle on a steam locomotive moves the train. 'The consciousness of brutes would appear to be related to the mechanism of their body simply as a collateral product of its working, and to be as completely without any power of modifying that working as the steam-whistle which accompanies the work of a locomotive engine is without influence upon its machinery.'[6]

A century later, the philosopher John Searle used another vivid metaphor, saying that, according to epiphenomenalists, human beings are like spume on the crest of a wave which thinks 'what a tough job it is pulling these waves up on the beach and then pulling them out again, all day long', and that our mental life is not 'any more important than a froth on the wave of physical reality'.[7] Whichever analogy you prefer, consciousness is just the noise made by the firing of neurons, no more the cause of action than sweat is the cause of a runner's exertion.

That the main threat to free will comes from materialism in general rather than from strict determinism can be seen in Nick Spencer's informative history of atheism, where time and again a denial of free will is part and parcel of the naturalistic world view which led people away from religion. One of the earliest examples of this is Lucretius, who in his first century BCE poem *De rerum natura* (*On the nature of things*) describes a universe governed purely by natural laws. In such a world, everything that happens is an effect of prior causes. And so he asked rhetorically, 'if ev'r all motions are co-linked, And from the old ever arise the new . . . Whence this free will for creatures o'er the lands, Whence is it wrested from the fates?'[8]

The same basic question again found no satisfactory answer when it was asked by European materialists at the dawn of the Enlightenment. Nature came to be seen as a kind of machine, and so human beings, as parts of nature, became mere cogs within it. Hence Jean Meslier, the eighteenth-century priest thought to be the first avowed atheist, wrote that: 'Man who believes himself free, is a fly who believes himself the master-motor in the machine of the universe, while he himself, without his own volition, is carried on by it.'[9] Similarly, Meslier's compatriot Baron d'Holbach wrote half a century later: 'Is not Nature herself a vast machine, of which the human species is but a very feeble spring?'[10] around the same time as the physician and philosopher Julien Offray de La Mettrie wrote a book called *Man a Machine* (*L'homme Machine*).[11]

Time and again, thinkers who have concluded that the universe is governed solely by natural laws have been quick to conclude that there is therefore no space for human freedom. That is the basic inference, and it depends not a jot on determinism, quantum theory or cutting-edge science to make or assess it. The fact that so many scientists appear to think otherwise reveals either philosophical naivety or a cynical exaggeration of the significance of their own research for ordinary life.

Just as the fundamental scientific challenge to free will has been the same for centuries, so the most common strategy to try to respond to it recurs in different guises. This strategy can be understood by analogy to an old problem in theology. Before science began to provide satisfactory accounts of how the universe worked, people would often attribute the workings of nature to God or gods. That is not to say that religion was nothing more than bad proto-science, or that all religions invoked deities in this way. But it would take a breathtakingly modernist rewriting of history to deny that the belief that divine powers directed nature was not extremely widespread.

As science began to mature, it became increasingly obvious that more and more of the workings of the world could be explained by natural laws alone. God seemed to be squeezed out of the picture. As Laplace reputedly said to Napoleon, explaining the absence of God in his account of the celestial movements, 'I have no need of that hypothesis.'

Unless you simply deny the science, you have only three options. You could give up belief in God. Alternatively, you could give up the idea that God is a kind of cosmic controller, pulling the levers that cause everything from the weather to the fall of a leaf. That is indeed what many theologians did, with more or less consistency. The third alternative, however, is to observe that science does not explain everything and to put your god in the gaps it leaves behind. The nineteenth-century evangelist Henry Drummond was the first to decry this strategy prominently in a lecture called 'The Ascent of Man'. 'There are reverent minds who ceaselessly scan the fields of Nature and the books of Science in search of gaps, gaps which they will fill up with God', he wrote. 'As if God lived in gaps?' Drummond could see that this was a dead end. 'If God is only to be left to the gaps in our knowledge, where shall we be when these gaps are filled up? And if they are never to be filled up, is God only to be found in the dis-orders of the world?'[12]

However, the God of the Gaps has endured. Although contemporary theologians always deny invoking this rearguard deity, he can be seen clearly in arguments that have him fine-tuning the fundamental constants of physics to ensure that humanity eventually emerges from the smoke of the big bang, or meddling with evolution to make sure we get the benefits of apparently improbable organs such as the eye.

In a very similar way, I believe we have hung onto an 'I of the gaps'. It became obvious a long time ago that we are essentially creatures of flesh and blood and that there is no non-physical ghost in the machine responsible for our thoughts, desires, beliefs and sensations. That is accepted even by many, perhaps most, theologians.[13] Yet the idea that all the richness of our inner lives and conscious thought is grounded in nothing more than physical stuff, cells not souls, makes no intuitive sense. So without necessarily formulating it as a coherent, conscious belief, people have refused to take physicalism to heart and have persisted with a conviction that something else is going on inside. It's not just that neurons fire and limbs move: somewhere in there is an 'I' pulling the levers. The alternative is too uncomfortable to contemplate: that 'I' am simply the sum of the levers moving.

Whenever the 'I of the gaps' is articulated explicitly, it is soon exposed as a hopelessly vague notion. But only a philosopher would be surprised that it is upon such nebulous beliefs that we often hang our lives. Asked to provide a coherent, comprehensive account of their fundamental religious, political or moral convictions, most people flounder, even often the more intelligent.

The 'I of the gaps' is a very old idea indeed, since the problem it seeks to solve became apparent as soon as a materialist understanding of the universe took hold. Hence in the first century Plutarch talked about how 'Some philosophers think they can free our impulses from being necessitated by external causes' by positing, as he opaquely put it, 'in the leading part of the soul an adventitious motion which becomes particularly evident in cases where things are indistinguishable'. What this means is that the soul has some capacity to intervene and determine the path of physical matter when forces in the physical world itself are in balance, such that a movement is not necessitated either way. The soul can tip the scales of nature when they are perfectly balanced. So, to offer an updated example, it might be that the laws of physics state that a neuron could fire or not fire, and in such cases, our free will could determine whether it did or not.

In Stoic philosophy this was known as the 'swerve'. 'For when two things are equivalent and equal in importance and it is necessary to take one of the two, there being no cause which leads us to one or the other since they do not differ from each other, the adventitious cause generates a swerve in the soul.'[14] However, this looks like a hopeless strategy for preserving the free self. Apart from the fact that the power to cause the swerve is completely mysterious, it appears to limit free will only to those rare cases in which nothing else is pushing us either way. Free will becomes supernature's way of dealing with nature's impasses.

Oddly enough, there are still those advocating something remarkably like the 'swerve' theory by trying to stuff free will into the gaps left by quantum indeterminacy. The Nobel Prize-winning scientist John C. Eccles is a notable example of this. In a paper co-written with Friedrich Beck in 1992, he saw the possibility of a non-material free will operating during exocytosis, 'the momentary opening of a channel in the presynaptic membrane' in the brain. Their hypothesis is that 'mental intention becomes neurally effective by momentarily increasing the probabilities for exocytoses'.[15]

There are also contemporary philosophers who, like Eccles, try to find space between the synapses where some non-physical willing can do its work. They postulate something called 'agent-causation'. The potential gap is prised open here because it is usually assumed that all causes are themselves effects of other, prior causes. This is what lies behind the worry that we are no more than elaborate machines, whose very actions are simply the result of causes beyond our control. But what if there is another kind of cause which is not itself a mere effect? Agent-causation, they suggest, is just such a cause.

Agent-causation is postulated as 'a special kind of causation of an action (or specifically of a free action) by an agent or person that cannot be reduced to or fully explained by causation of that action by events, processes and states of affairs involving the agent'.[16] That is the clearest definition I could find, and I don't think it's an accident that even that is pretty muddy because the concept itself appears to be extremely murky. What it adds up to is simply the proposal that human beings have some power to cause things to happen which is independent of all other forms of natural causation. In other words, it's free will as magic. Advocates of agent-causation go to great pains to argue that it is a coherent notion, not incompatible with our best scientific understanding. Likewise, there is nothing scientifically impossible about Eccles's hypothesis that a non-material free will operates during exocytosis. But more importantly, there is no positive evidence at all that some kind of hidden forces of will are at work in the brain. As the philosopher Tamler Sommers puts it, 'Possibility is cheap; actuality is expensive. It is the easiest thing in the world to suggest alternate explanations if you do not have to provide any positive support for them.'[17] It seems the only reason to think we must have such secret powers is the belief that we need them to save the notion of free will we want to save. The theory seems to be driven by the conclusion it is drafted in to support.

Another attempt to locate pure freedom in the gaps is contemporary philosopher Robert Kane's idea of 'self-forming actions'. Kane is aware of the problem that we make many decisions without conscious deliberation, and we make them on the basis of our characters, which it seems we did not ourselves shape. So to preserve responsibility for who we are and therefore the actions we perform, it would seem necessary to assert that at critical points in our lives we make free choices for ourselves, undetermined by the twin powers of nature and nurture, which shape the people we become. For reasons which I hope need no further explaining, most people would assume that this just isn't possible. Kane is more ambitious.

'Undetermined self-forming actions or SFAs occur at those difficult times of life where we are torn between competing visions of what we should do or become,' he writes. 'There is tension and uncertainty in our minds about what to do at such times, I suggest, that is reflected in appropriate regions of our brains by movement away from thermodynamic equilibrium – in short, a kind of "stirring up of chaos" in the brain that makes it sensitive to micro-indeterminacies at the neuronal level.'[18]

This is rather like the Stoic swerve. Sometimes it seems we really could decide either way, and even the brain is in a kind of state of suspension. At such times – *voila!* – we make free choices that make us the people we become. This seems to me a hopeless suggestion, which makes a desperate appeal to the most obscure and indeterminate areas of brain science, 'explaining' one mystery by positing another. So when he says, 'Some scientists have suggested that a combination of chaos and quantum physics might provide the genuine indeterminism one needs', I wonder, need for what?[19] 'Genuine indeterminism' is just that, and it has nothing to do with genuine freedom.

Agent-causation and self-forming actions seem to me to be just the latest doomed philosophical attempts to address worries that arise from accepting that brains are the engines of thought by looking for the gaps that science leaves behind. Academics may wish to argue over the details, but when a strategy is fundamentally flawed, you don't need to examine all its minutiae to know enough to abandon it.

That also holds with the most audacious gap theory of them all. Whereas the standard strategy is to find spaces in the material world into which non-physical causes can be slotted, Immanuel Kant attempted something far more ambitious.

21

Kant's argument is an intriguing one. Kant believed that the scientific world view makes free will impossible, and free will makes the scientific world view impossible. Given these two facts, there appear to be only two options: we either have to give up the notion of free will or the idea that the physical world, the world as it appears to us (in science as well as in everyday life), is the real world. Kant chose to save freedom rather than the reality of the physical world. He did this by proposing that the world as it appears to us, the world studied by science, is not the ultimate reality. We need to deny that the world of experience and perception is the world-in-itself if we are to assert the reality of freedom. As Kant put it, 'If appearances are things in themselves, freedom cannot be saved.'[20]

Kant therefore claimed that in addition to the phenomenal world – the world we experience and investigate scientifically – there is the noumenal world, the world as it is in itself. The nature of this noumenal world is almost completely unknown. Even time and space belong to the phenomenal world, not the noumenal one. Nonetheless, we are justified in believing that the noumenal world is where freedom of the will resides, because free will must be real, yet we can find no place for it in the phenomenal world. Hence there is no need to seek gaps in the physical world in which to slot free will; it can simply be relocated to the noumenal one. As Robert Kane explains it, free will is to be found in a '"noumenal self" outside space and time that could not be studied in scientific terms'.[21]

This is a form of reasoning known as a transcendental argument. Such arguments start from what we think must be the case and then work out what else must follow. There's nothing wrong with this in principle, but it becomes reckless when there is actually no evidence at all for what you claim must be the case. Kant as good as admits this audacity. 'By freedom,' he says, 'I mean the power to begin a state *on one's own*.' In 'this meaning of the term' Kant acknowledges that freedom 'is a pure transcendental idea' which 'contains nothing borrowed from experience'.[22]

It seems outrageous to me that Kant can argue with such disregard for empirical evidence. It leads him to attribute all sorts of causal powers to things in the noumenal world purely on the basis of speculation so that he can preserve cherished ideas about liberty and the power of thought. So Kant credits reason with the power to 'begin on its own a series of events. Reason begins the series in such a way that nothing begins in reason itself, but that reason, as unconditioned condition of any voluntary action, permits no conditions above itself.'[23] But postulating an unconditioned condition or uncaused cause is not to explain anything at all, but to replace one mystery with an even bigger one. Even Kant's followers sometimes admit as much. Schopenhauer, for example, chose Malebranche's dictum 'Freedom is a mystery' as both the epigraph and the conclusion of his Kant-inspired 1840 essay on free will.[24]

Perhaps the most decisive criticism of this 'I of the gaps' strategy is that it ends up diminishing precisely what it sets out to save. The goal is to find some kind of 'unmoved mover', a part of the self that can choose without having been caused to choose. Even if you could find such a thing, what you'd end up with is a kind of a magical homunculus, much smaller than the whole person whom it purportedly controls.

There is, I think, a reason why so many easily fall into this deflationary trap. Peter Hacker calls it 'the mereological fallacy': mistaking a whole for one or more of its parts.[25] When thinking about ourselves, we should be thinking about the whole of who we are, what it is that thinks, desires, feels and decides from moment to moment, brain and body, intellect and emotion. However, the I of the gaps strategy tries to locate a pocket of uncaused causation somewhere in the deep hidden recesses of the mind, which, even if it were there, would not be our free selves, but only a tiny part of our whole selves.

This is just one instance of a more general mistake. When looking for the source of free will, there is a tendency to look for some thing, which is the controller: the self, the soul, a part of the brain, a special faculty of the will. But no such thing exists, and even if it did, it would not be *us*. Worse, this quest for the part which frees the whole inevitably makes free will seem to disappear. Look at conscious control, for example, and you find that it is often absent, as automatic responses and decisions cause so many of our actions. Zoom in on brain events and you cannot see any thoughts doing work. Look at our rational deliberation and you find that it is often ignored by our emotional responses. Wherever you look, it seems the decisions are being taken elsewhere. And in a way they are: decisions are taken across the whole system, not just in one of its parts.

The mistake is a bit like watching a team sport, such as soccer, and trying to understand what is going on by following only one player at a time, trying to identify the one who is controlling the game. If you do that, all you'll see is someone running around looking elsewhere and only occasionally kicking a ball. This is in fact exactly what you see in the film *Zidane*, which tracks one of the best players in the world at the time, Zinedine Zidane, during one match. 'Following just one player instead of the ball, you lose all sense of the game', wrote the journalist Gary Younge.[26] In much the same way, looking at what one part of the self does rather than what the self is doing, you lose all sense of its agency.

In order to make sense of free will we have to abandon the tendency to talk of choices being made by our brains, or our minds, or our rational or conscious selves. We have to think of the agents of choice as being *us*: the whole people we are. These whole selves sometimes do things consciously, sometimes unconsciously; sometimes after thought, sometimes automatically; sometimes on the basis of reasons, sometimes on the basis of emotion or instinct. What makes us free is that, taken in the round, we have a sufficient amount

24

Central

of control over what we do. What that 'sufficient control' adds up to is in large part the subject of the rest of this book. But in order to find out what it is, we must start from the right point, which is to think of free will as something we have as whole persons, and not something a special, willing part of us has.

Matter needs a PR makeover. 'Materialism' is almost universally a dirty word. People complain that the consumerist society places too much emphasis on material objects, as though there were any other kind. There is, however, something else we should indeed place more value on: material subjects, that is, ourselves. But if we are to truly *Value* value ourselves for what we are, we have to fully embrace our materiality. The modern era can be characterised by, on the one hand, the growth of a materialist conception of the world and on the other, the Canute-like attempt to stop the materialist tide submerging humanity.

It is easy to see why we have been slow to embrace our physicality. A materialist world view appears to leave no place for human *agency* agency, seeing everything that happens as the result of physical laws playing themselves out. In vain do we look in the gaps of our scientific understanding to save our freedom. If we do, we will find the gaps will either close, contain only mystery or be too small for anything worth having to reside there.

So we have to accept that we are physical beings in a physical world, while resisting the temptation to locate our true selves in one of the parts that make us up. Facing up to this reality squarely, we can now turn to the more recent challenges to free will posed by neuroscience, and see if there is any way we can meet them and save our freedom.

PART TWO

Freedom Lost

2

The Neuroscientist

Imagine I asked you to tap a button whenever you liked. No one would force you to tap at any particular time, your finger would be entirely in your control and you would have no reason to prefer one time over another. Such an action would be the ultimate pointless free choice.

Now imagine I showed you what was going on in your brain during this experiment. You would see that the area of your brain involved in decision-making, the prefrontal cortex, would have fired up several milliseconds before you consciously thought of tapping the button. It might have seemed to you like a free, conscious choice, but it appears that your brain had made it first without your knowledge.

If this were just one experiment, it could be treated with some scepticism. But ever since the early 1980s when Benjamin Libet first seemed to show the brain initiating movements two hundred milliseconds before any conscious decision to make them, studies confirming his findings have piled up.[1] What's more, the gap between initiating the action and our conscious decision to act has lengthened. Time and again, neuroscientists have shown that when we make some choices, the conscious self is the last to know. The troubling conclusion drawn by many, including neuroscientist Sam Harris, is that 'the intention to do one thing and not another does not originate in consciousness – rather, it *appears* in consciousness'.[2]

Many interpreters of this and similar experiments see them as sounding the death knell for free will. For instance, Gabriel Kreiman of Harvard University detected electrical activity in areas of the brain involved in initiating movement (the supplementary motor area) and controlling attention and motivation (the anterior cingulate cortex) five seconds before volunteers were aware of their decision to press a button. 'There is no magic,' he told *New Scientist* in 2013. 'There are neurons, and there are ions that flow through membranes, and that is what is orchestrating our decisions. We don't need to invoke freedom.'[3]

If it is true that we begin to act before we consciously decide to act, then it would seem that conscious choices contribute precisely nothing to what we do. They are the epiphenomena described by T. H. Huxley: the empty noise made by the whirring of our brains.

The time-honoured strategy of invoking the I of the gaps has been used to try to address these concerns, strangely enough by Benjamin Libet himself. He did not want to believe that his experiments demonstrated that we had no free will, and he found a way to save something almost as good: 'free won't'. He thought that it was consistent with his findings that the conscious mind could intervene and 'veto' the actions which the brain had unconsciously initiated before we actually did them.

Others have looked for flaws, which suggest that the experiments are not quite as decisive as they appear to be. Neuroscientist David Eagleman, for example, has doubts about a 2009 version of the Libet experiments using fMRI scanners, which many took to confirm the original findings. He believes that the results were affected by the fact that the experimental subjects were trying to make sure their responses were as random as possible.

'It turns out that when we look at the fMRI signal, what we're finding is that the climbing activity before they actually hit the button is correlated with the relationship of what they're doing right now to what they did on the last trial,' he explained to me. In other words, people are asking themselves: am I waiting longer than I did last time? Am I acting more quickly than I did last time? And so on. This could be what the scanners are detecting before the conscious decision, not a prior unconscious decision. 'If this is correct,' says Eagleman, 'which I think it is, then what that means is there is still no killer experiment that demonstrates that we don't have free will.'

We might add to this the general worry that it requires a leap of faith to jump from conclusions about studies of people asked to make pointless choices in the lab to what they are doing when making meaningful life choices. Libet's experiments are very peculiar set-ups, and it is perhaps strange how quick people are to assume that they reveal anything at all about what real-life decision-making involves.

Nevertheless, it would be perilous to make any defence of free will hinge on the limitations of the experimental data so far. Given the wealth of research suggesting that much of what we do is unconscious, I would be very surprised if unconscious decisions did not precede conscious ones at least some of the time. To try to take comfort from the fact that the neuroscientific evidence isn't as conclusive as is often claimed is, I think, yet another misguided attempt to locate free will in the gaps of our scientific knowledge.

A robust defence of free will needs to address three components of the neuroscientific challenge to free will. The first is that our actions are caused by processes in the brain, not by thoughts and decisions. Second, that a great deal of what we do is not under our conscious control. Third, that although we often believe we could have done other than what we actually do, often, if not always, the brain casts the die before we're even aware we have a choice. To address these three challenges completely will require the rest of this book. But there are some things we can say already to at least blunt them.

In some ways, it is puzzling why so many are worried by the 'discovery' that actions in the body and thoughts in the mind can be traced back to events in the brain. Given that the brain plays a fundamental role in consciousness, wouldn't it be more surprising if *nothing* was going on in your brain before you made a decision? The philosopher Simon Blackburn says he's 'jolly glad' about Libet's findings since he 'would be very sorry to learn that my hand goes up without any antecedent events enabling it to happen'.[4] Similarly, the scientist Colin Blakemore asks, 'What else could it be that's making our muscles move if it's not our brains?' And what else could be making thoughts possible other than neurons firing? No one should pretend that we understand exactly how it is that physical brains give rise to conscious thoughts and perceptions, but nor should anyone doubt that in some sense they do.

However, because we don't yet understand the relationship between mind and brain, we don't yet know how to talk about it. For example, when describing the Libet experiments, it is very easy to talk about *your brain* deciding before *you* become aware of it, as though the brain were not a part of you. This is an example of the mereological fallacy we encountered in the previous chapter: the mistaking of parts and wholes. This way of talking can have important philosophical implications. The perfectly acceptable idea that *we make up our minds before we become aware that we have done so* becomes the disturbingly different idea that *our minds are made up for us, by our brains*.

The words and phrases we reach for when talking about the mind are often inadequate and misleading. For instance, I and others sometimes talk about brains 'causing' or 'giving rise to' thoughts and perceptions. That suggests that brains are doing all the real work and that thoughts and perceptions are in some sense mere effects of neural causes, which sounds very much like epiphenomenalism.

Do the scientific facts about brains require us to think of thoughts and actions in this way? I don't think they do. The undeniable fact is that brains provide the material means by which conscious life is sustained. Without brains there can be no human consciousness. But it does not follow from this that we can explain all human behaviour in neurological terms alone, and that conscious thoughts contribute nothing to our actions. That is a much stronger claim, which goes against the evidence of experience.

Take a simple example. I shout to you, 'Duck!' and you duck. Home in on the brain, and it may well be possible to trace a line of cause and effect which only describes sound waves entering your ear, translating into brain signals, in turn triggering further neural firings that lead to your muscles moving in such a way that you duck. We will not find embedded in any of this the meaning of the word 'duck'. However, it seems deeply implausible to suggest that we can make sense of what happened here unless we accept that the meaning of 'duck' had a vital role to play in the causal chain. If I had shouted 'Suck!', 'Cheese!' or 'Jump!', you would have reacted differently. We cannot then understand your behaviour unless we ascribe some critical importance to the meaning of 'duck'.

That can mean only one of two things: either the meaning of 'duck' had no role at all to play in your action, or a purely physical description of what went on would not provide a complete account of why you did what you did, adequate to explain what happened. Given how implausible the first option is, we should be very careful before rejecting the second.

The thesis we are questioning here can be summed up as the claim that *thoughts have no causal efficacy*: they do not affect what we do. 'Thoughts' should be understood very broadly here to include

meaning

Thought

not just beliefs, but also desires, intentions and simply the way in which we understand what we see and hear, like injunctions to duck.

When people deny the causal efficacy of thoughts, they often do so on the basis of experiments that at most show that thoughts do not affect actions in certain very specific actions. To jump to the general conclusion that thoughts *never* affect actions looks like a remarkable example of rash generalisation. The Libet experiments, for example, appear to show that conscious choice doesn't determine when we choose to move a finger in a laboratory situation. Even if this is true, it seems too much to leap from this to the claim that, for instance, the belief that immigrants are taking over the country is not a reason why a person voted for a nationalist political party. An experiment that shows that 'thoughts have no causal efficacy *here*' cannot show that 'thoughts have no causal efficacy *anywhere*'. That would be like claiming that because a person's religious belief does not affect their choice of soap powder, it doesn't affect their choice of spouse or place of worship.

The analogy is perhaps less exaggerated than you might think because, as a matter of fact, many experiments that appear to debunk the role of conscious thought in action focus on very specific kinds of action that are not particularly reason- or thought-based. The philosopher Shaun Nichols offered me as an example a famous study by John Bargh, in which subjects who were made to read passages that included words associated with old age subsequently walked more slowly than subjects who weren't.[5] None of these people were aware that they were altering their behaviour, or had any suspicion that what they had read was changing how they moved.

'Some people are shocked that people's behaviour can be affected so much by things they are unconscious of,' Nichols told me. But thoughts do not generally play a significant role in how we walk, unless we are deliberately acting or adjusting for some partic-ular reason. So typically, if you ask someone why they walked more slowly than usual to an elevator, they don't know. 'But what if you asked them, *why* did you walk to the elevator?' asks Nichols. 'It's not going to be like, "Jeez, I don't know, maybe it was to get out of the building?" They know why they walked to the elevator. If somebody is at an airline gate, and you say, "Why are you here?" they don't say, "Gee, I have no idea why I'm here."' No experiment has ever shown that people's beliefs have nothing to do with actions of this kind. So 'if you're going to draw big inferences about the nature of human decision-making from studies about the foibles, it's really important to keep in mind all of the things we do astonishingly well, so well that you could never publish an experiment because the editor would just say, "Well, of course people know that they're at the gate because they need to get a plane!"'

Work by the psychologists Kathleen Vohs and Jonathan Schooler also seems to show that thoughts do affect actions. Specifically, the belief that you have free will makes you act more morally, and the belief that you lack it makes you act less morally. In two experiments, they found that subjects who had read a passage which 'portrayed behaviour as the consequence of environmental and genetic factors' cheated more on a subsequent task than those who had read a neutral passage. They also found that 'increased cheating behaviour was mediated by decreased belief in free will'. Others have found similar results. This seems as clear an example as any of a belief affecting action.[6]

Perhaps the neatest and most powerful rejoinder to the idea that thoughts change nothing comes from the neuroscientist Dick Swaab, who dismisses free will out of hand as a 'pleasant illusion'. Nonetheless, in his book *We Are Our Brains* he reports that 'patients suffering from chronic pain can be coached to control activity in the front of the brain, thereby reducing their pain'. But hang on: if 'we are our brains' how can we control them? His own example is evidence that it is far too simplistic to talk as though our brains are doing all the work and conscious thought is redundant.[7]

35

For all the clever research showing how we are manipulated by unconscious processes, much of what we do is patently rooted in thoughts, reasons and beliefs. No credible scientific view of the mind can force the conclusion on us that thoughts have no role to play in guiding our actions. How they do so, however, is not so easy to explain. One possibility is that consciousness is somehow a property of physical stuff, whether it is a part of a brain or a table. If this were true, it would be odd if only some elements, like carbon, had this property. Therefore almost everyone who believes consciousness is a property of matter is a panpsychist, believing that mind or consciousness is a feature of all physical matter. Mind is everywhere.

This sounds crazy. Surely stones don't think? Well, no, and most panpsychists don't claim they do either. Only remarkably complicated physical structures like brains can think in any recognisable sense because thinking, as we know it, requires more complexity than the structure of the stone allows. Nonetheless, panpsychism does entail that there is some kind of trace of mind, some minimal subjective awareness, even in a pebble.

Many philosophers have ruled this possibility out because it seems that subjective awareness is just not the sort of thing that could ever be the property of brute matter. But maybe this is simply a lack of imagination. Matter may not be so brute after all, and believing that it is may be as ignorant and prejudiced as believing that 'brutes' like pigs and dogs cannot feel pain. The contemporary panpsychist Galen Strawson, for example, says that nothing in physics rules out the possibility that something physical cannot have experiences. 'To claim to know with certainty that spatio-temporal extension entails non-experientiality is to claim to know more about space-time than is warranted by anything in science.'[8] He accuses many materialists of being 'false naturalists' in the grip of 'the conviction that experience can't possibly be physical, that matter can't possibly be conscious'. Ironically, this is an assumption shared with Descartes's dualism, which asserts that the world is made up of two different substances, matter and mind. Indeed, it is doubly ironic because, as Strawson points out, 'Descartes was at bottom aware that one can't rule out the possibility that matter may be conscious. Many of the false naturalists, by contrast, have no such doubts.'[9]

Strawson may be right about this. Weirdness is not, after all, a sure sign of falsity. As biologist J. B. S. Haldane famously said, 'the Universe is not only queerer than we suppose, but queerer than we can suppose'.[10] That may be so, but many, including myself, find it very hard even to understand what the panpsychist claim really adds up to. The choice, it seems, is between a view that is ludicrous and one that is empty, as Colin McGinn put it.[11] If it is the claim that stones think, it is ludicrous. If it is the claim that any atom could be part of something that does think, then it is empty, because this is what anyone who thinks brains are required for consciousness believes. So although panpsychism cannot be ruled out, it remains an explanation of last resort for the consciousness of physical beings.

A more promising alternative appeals to the idea of different levels of explanation. To take a mundane example, when I hit the '#' key on my keyboard, a '#' symbol appears on my screen. There must be some explanation of this at the very lowest, subatomic level, involving nothing more than chain reactions between electrons, neutrons and protons. That might appear to be the most fundamental explanation of all. But of course it isn't the only one, and for practical purposes it isn't the best. Far preferable is the one that refers to the code written into the computer software. When I press the key, a digital signal is sent which passes through a program, resulting finally in a digital signal, which 'tells' the monitor which pixels to blacken out. To say that the 'real' explanation is the subatomic one and that the existence of code does nothing to explain what happens would not just be wrong but perverse.

When it comes to our minds and behaviour, there are explanations at the level of conscious thought, the biochemical brain and of fundamental physics. If we took seriously the reductionist idea that the only true explanation of why things happen is to be found at the most basic, lowest level, then not even brain science would be 'really' explaining behaviour. Physics rather than psychology or neuroscience provides the ultimate reductionist account of why things happen.

We do not have to decide which among atoms, brains or thoughts provide the 'real' explanation for what we do. We simply need to accept that there are different accounts we can give at each level, and which is most appropriate depends on what we are trying to understand or explain. This notion of appropriateness can be understood in a purely pragmatic sense. You could believe in principle that a physicist with powers of Laplacian omniscience could describe everything that a person has done on the basis of physical information alone. But because in practice this is never going to be possible, you might accept that we still have use for the explanations of psychologists and neuroscientists.

However, there is increasing evidence that scientific explanations don't work as neatly as this after all. The old reductionist paradigm was that the way to understand how anything works is to break it down until you get to the most fundamental processes. In other words, the complex whole can be entirely explained through the workings of the simpler parts. This has commonly been understood to imply the theoretical possibility of reconstructing from the bottom up as well as deconstructing from the top down: if you know what the atoms are doing, you'll know what the larger objects made up of them will do. But the Nobel Prize-winning physicist Philip W. Anderson suggests this is a widespread mistake. 'The reductionist hypothesis,' he says, 'does not by any means imply a "constructionist" one: the ability to reduce everything to fundamental laws does not imply the ability to start from those laws and reconstruct the universe. In fact, the more the elementary particle physicists tell us about the nature of the fundamental laws, the less relevance they seem to have to the very real problems of the rest of science, much less to those of society.'[12]

Science increasingly seems to be confirming the old adage that the whole is greater than the sum of its parts. For instance, you can look at how the brain works and in theory describe everything that goes on in terms of fundamental particles. But you cannot look only at the laws governing the behaviour of particles and from that work out what will happen when they are arranged into complex organs like brains. The laws of physics do not predict consciousness, yet that is what the physical universe gives rise to.

To put it another way, systems behave in ways that cannot be predicted simply by knowing the behaviour of the elements of the system. Systems acquire characteristics that their component parts do not have. A swarm of bees can be deadly even though no bee in it is lethal; an orchestra can play a piece of discordant music even though each instrument by itself is playing harmoniously; five functional human beings can form a dysfunctional group. As another Nobel Prize-winning physicist Robert Laughlin put it, 'what we are seeing is a transformation of world view in which the objective of understanding nature by breaking it down into ever smaller parts is supplanted by the objective of understanding how nature organises itself'.[13]

This new understanding is known as complexity theory 'A complex system is composed of many different systems that interact and produce emergent properties that are greater than the sum of their parts and cannot be reduced to the properties of their constituent parts,' as the scientists Grégoire Nicolis and Catherine Rouvas-Nicolis put it.[14] Or, to take psychologist Michael Gazzaniga's account of 'emergent properties', micro-level complex systems 'self-organise . . . into new structures, with new properties that pre-viously did not exist, to form a new level of organisation at the macro level'. In 'strong' versions of this theory, 'the new property is irreducible, is more than the sum of its parts, and because of the amplification of random events, the laws cannot be predicted by an underlying fundamental theory or from an understanding of the laws of another level of organisation'.[15]

To give a clear example: if this is correct, quantum physics is more fundamental than Newtonian physics, but Newton's laws can't be torn up and replaced by quantum laws. 'Classical properties, such as shape, viscosity, and temperature, are just as real as the quantum ones, such as spin and nonseparability,' says Gazzaniga.[16]

Gazzaniga is interested in how complexity provides a way of understanding how minds operate in ways that can't be either pre-dicted or understood by studying only brain processes. Mind and consciousness are 'emergent properties' which arise out of nothing more than brain processes, because the complex organisation of these processes creates new properties not found at the fundamental phys-ical level.

This explains how it can be that beliefs, desires and intentions can actually change things, without us having to think that they are mysterious, non-physical things. 'Mental states that emerge from our neural actions do constrain the very brain activity that gave rise to them,' explains Gazzaniga. 'Mental states such as beliefs, thoughts, and desires all arise from brain activity and in turn can and do influ-ence our decisions to act one way or another.'[17]

This is one of the most important scientific facts we need to bear in mind when thinking about free will. Too often it can seem that, if brains are the engines of thought, then thoughts themselves cannot change anything. Complexity theory shows us how this can be false, without the need to postulate any strange, weird, supernatural or non-physical will or soul. It shows that the idea that thoughts, beliefs and desires can cause things to happen is not outmoded metaphysics, but bang up-to-date science.

I'm fairly sure that the right way to understand the apparently self-evident fact that thoughts do change what we do will involve thinking about levels of explanation rather than adopting panpsychism. I'm less sure whether that will be because we cannot in practice do without explanations at the psychological level or because we cannot in principle explain everything at the most fundamental physical level. My bet would be on the latter, or a third possibility I can't even imagine. However this debate resolves itself, we already understand enough to see that accepting that in some sense our thoughts and actions are only possible because of our brains should not trouble us. Neuroscience is filling in details of the naturalist picture, but there is plenty of room for human agency in it.

There is another way of understanding how thoughts have efficacy without thinking of them as causes at all. The Austrian philosopher Ludwig Wittgenstein made an important distinction between reasons and causes. We can think of an action as being simply a consequence of the grand chain of causation that goes back to the big bang. But there's another sense in which human action is very clearly produced by reasons, and you can't properly understand why someone has done something unless you understand the reasons for it.

For example, if I turn on the light, the cause of it coming on is the movement of my hand, which flicked a switch and turned on an electrical current. But the reason for the movement is that I wanted to find my book. Similarly, the cause of the thousands of deaths at Hiroshima was the explosion of an atomic bomb; the reason was the desire to bring a swift end to the Pacific war. Reasons and causes both explain why things happen, but in very different ways.

The philosopher Harry Frankfurt supports this broad way of looking at things, saying: 'When we say what the reason is, we're not

Explanation

identifying the cause of the action – the cause of the action has got to be something physiological. A reason is not that, although the reason itself also has a physiological counterpart or foundation. The reason is something else: it explains or identifies why we want to perform the action.'

So, as I suggested to Frankfurt across a transatlantic phone line, as long as there's a meaningful sense in which you can say 'he did it because . . .' and what follows is a reason, worries about determinism are misguided. No matter what's true about determinism, we have reasons for actions and we have reasons for behaviour.

'What you're saying,' replied Frankfurt, 'is that when the question is raised, "Why did he do it?" there are two kinds of answers that could be given to that, and the people who are concerned about determinism are concerned only about one of those types of answer. Yeah, I think that's a fair way of putting it.'

The point here cannot be that reasons have no role to play in the causal story, otherwise they become yet more epiphenomena. The point is rather that reasons are not events, as causes are. Nonetheless, things that are not events are often critical parts of the causal story. Striking a match will only start a flame if oxygen is present, and the presence of oxygen is not an event. In a similar way, most of what we do is for a reason, but those reasons are not the actions or events that trigger what we do.

Even if we do satisfy ourselves that thoughts can affect actions, there still seems to be another, potentially more serious challenge to our understanding of free will from contemporary neuroscience. It has shown how much of what we do is outside of our conscious control. We should have known long ago that the brain is behind every thought we have. But perhaps we also believed that, nonetheless, the thoughts that really did the moving were the conscious ones. We've already seen a challenge to this in Libet's experiments, but there is a lot of other work that has suggested the conscious mind does less than we commonly assume.

Some of this evidence is genuinely disturbing. Take, for instance, the previously entirely normal American schoolteacher who began secretly visiting child pornography websites and soliciting prostitutes at massage parlours. His behaviour eventually led him to court, where a judge gave him the opportunity to change his ways. But he failed to complete a Sexaholics Anonymous programme, making sexual advances to the women on it. Before he could start his prison sentence, however, he was admitted to hospital complaining of terrible headaches. In turned out he had an egg-sized brain tumour, and while remanded in psychiatric care, he had an operation to have it removed. His deviant behaviour stopped.[18]

Was it really so simple that the tumour had caused his paedophilia? It might not be quite that straightforward, but neurologists who have studied the case saw confirming evidence of the growth's role when several months later the headaches and the disturbing behaviour returned. It was found that so too had his tumour. It was removed once more and again, he returned to normal. Throughout all this experience, his conscious mind was unaware of what was driving his desires and actions.

Much of what we do in ordinary life is also not under conscious control, because we do it before we're even aware we're doing it. 'Our conscious awareness is the mere tip of the iceberg of nonconscious processing,' as Michael Gazzaniga puts it. More troubling still, 'Because consciousness is a slow process, whatever has made it to consciousness has already happened. It is a fait accompli.'[19] Such is the body of evidence for this that neuroscientist Patrick Haggard says that: 'The dominant view at the moment in the field is that our experience of agency is really just a narrative that we make up after the event to explain all the scrapes and situations that we get ourselves into.'[20]

David Eagleman also believes that the vast majority of our thinking is unconscious and has discovered that many people find that very disturbing, even though he says: 'I don't find it disturbing at all.' For instance, he tells me: 'I was talking to a film director at one point who got so angry that he stood up at the table and screamed and yelled and said, "Are you saying that my decisions and choices are not mine?" And I said, "Look, they belong to you, but they're not always consciously deliberated."'

Why should we be bothered by the thought that our unconscious minds do so much of the work? Why should we believe that only *conscious* thoughts can lead to free choices? Not even all the neuroscientists whose work undermines the belief that our conscious minds are in control believe this. For example, John-Dylan Haynes, a neuroscientist at the Bernstein Center for Computational Neuroscience in Berlin, found a seven-second gap between the initiation of an action and conscious awareness of it. But he did not think that that meant subjects didn't choose to act. 'My conscious will is consistent with my unconscious will – it's the same process,' he told *New Scientist*.[21]

There are many things going on in our brains that we are not aware of. Even with a naive view of free will, conscious choices involve a lot of things we are not at all aware of. We have no subjective sense, for instance, of how a decision to kick a ball translates itself into electrochemical activity in the brain and body and ultimately muscle movement. We may want something and not know why we want it, even though there are historical, social and biological reasons. If we demand that free choices have to be fully conscious choices, don't we set the bar too high?

Try to monitor yourself for a day. How many of your decisions and actions are preceded by a conscious decision? And how many of those are preceded by conscious deliberation? I don't think I'm unusual in finding that decisions emerge more often than they are fully worked out consciously. Faced with a choice of drinks, for instance, my decision is often simultaneous with my announcement of it. Indeed, sometimes if I can't decide what to order at a restaurant, hearing what I say when the waiter asks is a deliberate strategy for resolving my indecision.

Even when we think about more intellectual matters, answers often just pop out. Consider trying to find the solution for a crossword clue: 'electronic union arises'. Often you will run through some thought processes consciously: six letters . . . starts with an e . . . fourth letter r . . . another word for 'arise'? . . . But when the answer comes, it does so in an instant, seemingly of its own accord. 'Emerge!' Only then do you see: e-merge.

'How can I tell what I think till I see what I say?' as E. M. Forster perceptively put it.[22] We should not need neuroscience to tell us that our conscious minds are often the last to know what we're thinking. Daily experience shows us just the same thing. If we attend to what is going on when we think, what we normally find is a complete absence of any awareness of where thoughts come from. One common Buddhist meditation, for example, is to attend to your thoughts, feelings and sensations so that you notice them simply 'arising'. You do have some conscious control over how much you choose to endorse or attend to them, but you do not control their happening.

Why then is it that people tend to assume that the cause of their thoughts and actions is often their own conscious self, when they are not actually conscious of any self causing action? Two notable philosophers have suggested that the answer is to be found in the very fact that we do not observe any causal power at work.

Given that we intuitively understand that nothing happens without a cause, when we notice that we are doing things and we are not aware of anything else causing them, we assume we ourselves are filling the causal gap. 'Men believe that they are free,' wrote Spinoza, 'precisely because they are conscious of their volitions and desires; yet concerning the causes that have determined them to desire and will they do not think, not even dream about, because they are ignorant of them.'[23] In other words, having no idea about the physical brain processes which produce our thoughts and actions, we just assume we must have produced them ourselves by an act of will.

Hume advocated a similar view. He thought that when we look out into the world, we have a kind of instinct to attribute some necessary connection between a physical event and its cause, even though we never actually observe it. You see the lightning strike the tree and the tree bursting into flames, but strictly speaking you do not see the lightning setting the tree alight. You only observe one thing after another, and it is your mind that connects them with ideas of causation. We are similarly under-informed when we consider our own actions. 'When again they turn their reflections towards the operations of their own minds,' writes Hume, 'and feel no such connexion of the motive and the action; they are thence apt to suppose, that there is a difference between the effects which result from material force, and those which arise from thought and intelligence.'[24] In other words, unable to discern a physical cause for our thoughts and actions, yet believing everything has some kind of cause, we attribute a different kind of causation, one that originates in the mind.

Hume and Spinoza both advocate variants of the same intriguing idea, that we don't really have a strong *feeling* of a free will at all. Rather, because we do not believe that things just happen, free will becomes a kind of causal Polyfilla, used to fill the gap between the causes of our choices that we are ignorant of and a causal story sufficient to explain why we actually do what we do.

This is a counter-intuitive view, since it is often taken to be obvious that we actually 'feel' as though we act freely and consciously. However, the truth is rather that 'we do not feel as free as we think we do', as Sam Harris puts it.[25] Harris is right, but when he claims that this means 'we are not the authors of our thoughts and actions *in the way that people generally suppose*',[26] he fails to emphasise that last caveat, where the italics are all mine. There seems no good reason to think of actions that do not follow from rational deliberation as being any less ours. We do not, for example, think actions that flow from our feelings are less ours than ones that flow from thought. As Aristotle asked rhetorically about mistakes, 'How are errors that express emotion any less voluntary than those that express rational calculation? For both sorts of errors are to be avoided; and since non-rational feelings seem to be no less human [than rational calculation], actions resulting from emotion or appetite are also proper to a human being; it is absurd, then, to regard them as involuntary.'[27] Our actions are no less free when they flow from our feelings as when they flow from our thoughts, so long as both those thoughts and feelings are our own.

One final reason why people should not be too concerned by the discovery that much of what we do is unconscious is captured in what I call the quantitative fallacy. This is the mistake of thinking that what is crucial is the mere quantity of a particular factor, rather than its quality. For example, humans share 85 per cent of our DNA with zebra fish. But that 15 per cent difference is absolutely critical. Similarly, so what if 99 per cent of our cognitive processing is unconscious? It might still be true that the tiny fraction that is conscious is of vital importance. Indeed, it is surely essential, if our thinking is to do any important work, that our conscious minds are not kept busy working out trivial everyday things like which direction to turn a door handle or what the correct speed to stir a coffee is.

I'll be expanding on the role of the unconscious in free action in the chapters to come. There is more to be said about what it means to choose freely if it does not mean to choose consciously. For now it should be enough to note that to insist free choice always requires conscious deliberation is to demand more than even our subjective experience suggests we need.

Let's say you accept that your choices and deliberations depend in some way on brain events and that not all of these need to be conscious in order for you to be free. Still, there does seem to be something else that is troubling about the picture of action that emerges from the materialist world view, brought into sharp focus by recent neuroscience. That is to say, it rather looks like whatever you do, in a sense you had to do it. You could not have done otherwise.

The body and brain are a physical system. At any point in time, it is in a given physical state, which includes the state of the environment around it. From that state, according to the laws of physics, it has to behave in a certain way. Just as a rubber ball hitting the ground has to bounce and can't carry on through it, just as a dropped rock must fall and will not float in thin air, so every single neuron must fire or not fire according to its state and what is going on around it. So at any set point, we cannot do other than what we in fact do. To claim otherwise is to claim that we can defy the laws of nature, make physical objects immune to physical causes.

Imagine a snapshot of your brain as you consider a proposal of marriage. Your brain is in a certain state and is wired up in a certain way. When it processes the stimulus of your beloved asking, 'Will you marry me?' it is bound to process it in a certain way.

This seems just as true if you look at the brain at the functional level rather than that of fundamental physics. The computer analogy may be overworked when it comes to the brain, but there is a sense in which all your beliefs and desires are now part of a program, the software that runs on the hardware of the brain. Given all this, surely it is not open to the brain to generate just any response? Indeed, it is bound to generate only one.

The only caveat to this provides little comfort. There may be some indeterminacy in the brain's operations, a kind of luck factor which means that sometimes one decision is made, sometimes another. But as we have already seen, randomness does not introduce the kind of freedom of choice we want. Whether our decisions flow inevitably from the state of the brain or there is some random fluctuation, it remains true that it was not within our own power to have decided otherwise. It might seem to us that we could have accepted or rejected the proposal, but we couldn't have.

This point is worth stressing, since it is often mistakenly believed that an escape from inevitability provides a way back for free will. But as Sam Harris starkly puts the challenge in the context of responsibility: 'Either our wills are determined by prior causes and we are not responsible for them, or they are the product of chance and we are not responsible for them.' Actions that happen by chance are no more the product of our wills than ones that happen as the result of a deterministic chain of cause and effect.

This presents a major threat to our received idea of free will. Surely if free will means anything it is that I can choose other than how I actually choose? This certainly seems to be central to the common sense idea of free will. Shaun Nichols is a philosopher who is interested in finding out what people's philosophical intuitions are, rather than assuming he just knows. I met him in a London restaurant, which provided a stock example of everyday free will: I ordered the goat, but surely I could just as well have ordered the halibut. This strong intuition of alternative possibilities appears to take a grip very early in life. Nichols told me about experiments with children where they saw a ball roll to the bottom of a box and a person touch the bottom of a box. Whereas the kids recognised that the rolling ball could not have done otherwise, 'even four-year-old children will say a person could have done something else', he told me.

With adults, you can ask the more precise question of whether someone, say, 'could have chosen a different dish even if everything else had been the same right up to the instant when he made the choice'. If you do, says Nichols, you find that 'adults tend to give the indeterminist answer and say, yeah, even if things had been exactly the same right up until the moment of choice, they could have done something different'.

This appears to be central to how people conceive of their own free will. In one experiment, Nichols and his colleagues explain to participants what determinism means, without using that word. They check that they have understood and basically kick out any who still don't get it after a few tries. Those that are left then have to make a choice, such as which charity to give to. The question they are then asked is, if determinism were true, would the way it felt to make the decision turn out to have been mistaken? And 'people hugely say that it would be, that determinism is inconsistent with the way their choices feel'.

So the 'could have done otherwise' intuition appears to be very strong and important for our common conception of free will. But why, and should it be? Take the 'why' question first. Even if determinism is true, David Eagleman rightly says: 'There's a very real sense in which I have made choices when I'm at the buffet.' But 'I guess the point that bothers people is that if you rewound history a hundred times and put me in front of that buffet, I'd make that same decision every time. Why does that frustrate people? I guess it's because we want to believe that we can behave otherwise, that given some situation we're not slaves to the situation and our past.'

That's a natural way of putting it, perhaps, but 'slave' is a loaded and misleading word. To say you're a slave in this case is simply to say that when you go to that buffet you make that choice on the basis of a combination of your settled preferences over time, what's available there right now, what you feel like at that moment, your beliefs about what you should have. All these things interact and generate a decision. Is that being a slave? What would it mean to be less of a slave? People surely don't think it would be a good thing if you just chose randomly. You don't want the freedom to have chosen prunes, which you don't like. It seems people are looking for something between being determined beings and capricious generators of random choices. But what does that add up to: the capacity to have taken one sausage and two rashers of bacon, instead of two sausages and one rasher? To ignore all your preferences, beliefs and desires and take the black pudding just because you can? Why would that be valuable?

Once again, the best way to think about this is to forget about neuroscience for a moment and just attend to the experience of lived life. If someone proposes to you, in what sense is it true that you are free to say yes or no? Unless it is a forced marriage, there is no one compelling you to answer one way or the other. Nonetheless, given the way you feel about the person, your desires, your values and plans, isn't it inevitable that you will answer one way or the other? Of course, you may be ambivalent and undecided, but all that means is that it is inevitable you will not be able to make a clear choice. Whatever is true of you and the proposer at the time, isn't it inevitable that you respond the way you do, be that with joy, alarm or anguish?

Put it another way. Someone you really don't want to marry proposes to you. Obviously, you turn them down. So in what way was it true that you could have done otherwise, that you could have said, 'I will'? Nothing was physically preventing you from doing this, but clearly it was just not a live option. You were bound to reply the way you did. There's no need to invoke neuroscience or the laws of physics to reach that conclusion.

David Hume concluded more or less the same a good few hundred years ago. 'The conjunction between motives and voluntary actions is as regular and uniform as that between the cause and effect in any part of nature,' he wrote. Human actions flow as inexorably from the characters of the actors as water flows inexorably from the source of a river. The only reason why we do not acknowledge this is that we do not feel any compulsion to act as we do. Our actions appear optional to us because the forces that make them inevitable are not evident to us.

To see why we should not find this disturbing, imagine what would be the case if it were not true. If our choices and actions were not the product of our characters, situations, histories and dispositions then we would become unpredictable – random, even – in our behaviour. When you choose a drink, for example, you do so because you have certain tastes and preferences. This makes your choices somewhat predictable. But if your choices did not flow from your beliefs and preferences, then they would be merely capricious. That would appear to make you free only in the sense that a balloon let loose in the sky is free to be blown where the wind takes it.

To freely accept a proposal of marriage is not to make a choice that you believe you could equally have made otherwise. It is rather to embrace the only choice that really seems worth taking to you, free from any coercion from another. To freely choose a cup of coffee is simply to act on the preference you have at the time, not to decide what that preference is.

When we do get a clearer sense that we could have chosen otherwise, that usually adds up to no more than a realisation that other options have their attractions, and that in other circumstances you may have chosen differently. It is not to say that at that particular time you really could have chosen other than as you did. For example, one day you take a tea rather than your customary coffee. Why? Because you are not a blind creature of habit, and you observe that you actually fancy a change today and are not compelled to always do what you usually do, even if in one sense on each occasion you are compelled to do what you actually do.

Whatever the complete explanation, our strong intuitive conviction that we are not compelled at any given point to do what we do on the basis of what has happened up until that point seems to be highly dubious. But it is not obvious that this delivers any fatal blow to our belief in free will. Indeed, it is perfectly compatible with it, as I will attempt to show later.

Another reason why many people are troubled by the thought that we cannot do other than what we actually do is that they mistakenly assume this would mean that everything was fated or predestined. Fate or destiny is the idea that, no matter what we try to do, we will end up where we are preordained to end up. Destiny is a kind of external force that guides nature along a predetermined course.

There's a wonderful example of how helpless we would be if this were true in Tom Stoppard's play *Rosencrantz and Guildenstern Are Dead*. On a boat to England, Rosencrantz is overcome by the feeling that he is being pushed around by a fate he cannot control. He longs to escape this bondage and, looking over the side of the ship, he says, 'I could jump over the side. That would put a spoke in their wheel.' But then Guildenstern adds, 'Unless they're counting on it.' Rosencrantz changes his mind: 'I shall remain on board. That'll put a spoke in their wheel.' Stoppard's next stage direction says it all: *The futility of it, fury*. If we are pawns of destiny, then nothing we can do can change anything, as even attempts to alter fate are already part of our fate.

The inescapability of the laws of physics, however, does not entail this kind of predetermination. Indeed, it denies it. There is no external author of destiny that forces nature's hand. Rather, nature simply unfolds. Given the indeterminacy implied by quantum theory, it is probably impossible to know in advance how it will eventually unfold. Nonetheless, it does so, and at each moment what happens next is purely the result of what has happened so far.

Rosencrantz is right to think that he can only do what he goes on to do, but not that this is because the script of his life has already been written. He is pushed by the past, not pulled by his predestined future.

Although the difference between fate and not being to able to do other than what we do seems clear, people do appear to get them confused. The root of this appears to be a failure to distinguish between the idea that at any given time we are bound to choose what we in fact choose, and the idea that our choices make no difference to what happens. Sometimes the way philosophers speak encourages this misconception. Saul Smilansky, for instance, calls determinism 'the mere unfolding of the given', a phrase which suggests impotence on the part of the agent.[28]

But as P. F. Strawson puts it, 'It is not a consequence of any general thesis of determinism which might be true that nobody knows what he's doing or that everybody's behaviour is unintelligible in terms of conscious purposes or that everybody lives in a world of delusion or that nobody has moral sense.'[29] Even Sam Harris, the most fervent denier of free will, says: 'the fact that our choices depend on prior causes does not mean that they don't matter', and so 'Human choice ... is as important as fanciers of free will believe.'[30]

There is compelling evidence that people too easily assume determinism is the same as fatalism and that this makes them more inclined to oppose compatibilism: the view that free will is compatible with determinism. (In the contemporary free will debate, determinism is usually taken to mean the belief that everything is governed by physical laws, whether or not that makes everything that happens inevitable in the Laplacian sense of the term.) The philosopher Eddy Nahmias suspected that people 'may assume that determinism entails that psychological processes ... are *bypassed* by other causal processes'. That would mean that 'the agent would end up doing what she does regardless of what she had thought or wanted or decided'.[31] Determinism is often said to entail that what happens 'has to happen', but people may take this to mean 'everything has to happen *no matter what*'. As we have seen, none of this follows. 'Determinism does not in fact entail bypassing,' says Nahmias. 'Determinism does not mean that agents' desires, beliefs and decisions have no effect on what they do.'[32] Determinism does not mean that our decisions don't change anything, simply that our decisions can't be changed.

Nahmias had a testable hypothesis: 'the more one interpreted a description of determinism to involve bypassing, the less one would attribute free will'. One clever experiment tested this out. Half of the participants were presented with a description of determinism that was couched entirely in neurological terms (I have italicised these), at the level of the brain. 'Most respected *neuroscientists* are convinced that eventually we will figure out exactly how all of our decisions and actions are entirely caused,' it said. 'For instance, they think that whenever we are trying to decide what to do, the decision we end up making is completely caused by the *specific chemical reactions and neural processes* occurring in our *brains*. The *neuroscientists* are also convinced that these *chemical reactions and neural processes* are completely caused by our current situation and the earlier events in our lives, and that these earlier events were also completely caused by even earlier events, eventually going all the way back to events that occurred before we were born.' It goes on to explain how, if this is right, 'once specific earlier events have occurred in a person's life, these events will definitely cause specific later events to occur'.

The other half were presented with an identical text, except that instead of neuroscientists there were psychologists, and instead of brain processes, there were thoughts, beliefs, and so on. So it read: 'Most respected *psychologists* are convinced that eventually we will figure out exactly how all of our decisions and actions are entirely caused. For instance, they think that whenever we are trying to decide what to do, the decision we end up making is completely caused by the specific *thoughts, desires, and plans* occurring in our minds,' and so on.

The reason this is so clever is that in both scenarios, what we end up doing is described as equally inevitable. The only difference is that the second version makes it clear that thoughts, beliefs, and so on are playing a role, whereas the first, by only talking of brain events, leaves open the possibility that conscious thought has no role to play at all and is completely bypassed by neural events, which is what many take it to mean. As predicted, when the scenario is described in psychological terms, 83 to 89 per cent of respondents say that the agent acted of their own free will, that their decisions were up to them, that they were morally responsible for their actions and that they deserve praise and blame. When it is described in neurological terms, however, only 39 to 52 per cent agree with these statements. This seems convincing evidence that it is not belief in determinism per se which leads many people to reject free will; it is belief in a kind of fate where we do what we do whatever we think, believe or decide. Nahmias has gone to some pains to make sure that his experimental subjects really do understand that, in the scenarios he presents to them, people could not have done otherwise. He has also conducted other experiments that point in the same direction.

This turns conventional wisdom concerning intuitions about free will on its head. In the philosophical literature on free will, it is often asserted, as though it were self-evident fact, that people are naturally incompatibilists who do not believe free will and determinism can coexist. That places the onus of proof on compatibilists – who believe free will and determinism can coexist – to show why it is that we can have free will if in some important sense we could not have done otherwise. Nahmias's work suggests that, on the contrary, when people properly understand what compatibilism means, they tend to endorse it. 'Genuine incompatibilists,' he says, 'represent a very small minority of the folk.' That doesn't make compatibilism correct, of course, but it does shift the burden of proof, and demonstrates that compatibilism is not a kind of subtle evasion that only philosophers would believe, but closer to common sense than was previously believed, 'at most a slightly revisionary theory rather than a significant revolution'. And what is true here of compatibilism is also true of any view, which, while denying the inevitability of strict determinism, accepts that at the time of acting, no one can do other than they do.

The question of whether people are intuitive compatibilists or incompatibilists may, however, be the wrong one. The problem is that you can ask people whether they agree or disagree with statements such as 'if determinism is true then people aren't responsible', but as Shaun Nichols points out, 'that thought for most people was never part of their normal cognition. It just turns out that if you ask them on reflection this is what they'll say. Incompatibilism is not explicit in their thought.'

Too many philosophically naive neuroscientists and their champions have claimed more than their findings permit. Many are engaged in what I'd call the Neo-Laplacian Project of finding the physical, neural causes of beliefs and actions. This leads to a version of the old problem that to a hammer, everything looks like a nail. If you look for the neural causes of action, then the only causes of action you'll find are neural ones, and it is a natural though illogical leap to conclude that therefore these are the only causes of action.

Understanding why the challenge to free will of brain science is overstated has allowed us to identify clearly three assumptions that may lead us astray when thinking about free will: that a free choice must not be determined or even too conditioned by its past causes; that free choice has to be the result of a conscious decision; and that to choose freely it must always have been possible that you could have done otherwise. I have tried to show how all three are highly questionable, and by the end of this book I hope to have shown that all three are actually false. I'll be arguing for a positive idea of human freedom which does not require an escape from the laws of physics, for all free choices to be conscious, or for the possibility of doing other than we do.

This positive account needs to explain why people like the man whose brain tumour turned him into a paedophile is different from the rest of us, whose actions are in some sense no less driven by the workings of the brain. This is something I'll return to later when discussing the case of the psychopath.

For now, it is sufficient to have shown that nothing in brain science is fatal to free will. However, might there be another, more threatening challenge? Could our choices be written not in the stars or the brain, but in our genes?

3

The Geneticist

Whenever you read stories about identical twins separated at birth, they tend to follow the narrative template set by the most remarkable of them all: the 'two Jims'. James Springer and James Lewis were separated as one-month-olds, adopted by different families and reunited at age thirty-nine. When University of Minnesota psychologist Thomas Bouchard met them, he found, as a *Washington Post* article put it, both had 'married and divorced a woman named Linda and remarried a Betty. They shared interests in mechanical drawing and carpentry; their favorite school subject had been math, their least favorite, spelling. They smoked and drank the same amount and got headaches at the same time of day.' The similarities were numerous and uncanny. A great deal of who they would turn out to be appears to have been written in their genes.

Other studies at the world-leading Minnesota Center for Twin and Family Research suggest that many of our traits are more than 50 per cent inherited, including leadership, traditionalism or obedience to authority; a sense of well-being and zest for life; alienation; vulnerability or resistance to stress; fearfulness or risk-seeking; and the capacity for becoming rapt in an aesthetic experience. Other researchers have suggested that even when it comes to central issues of religion, life partner selection and politics, our choices are much more determined by our genes than we think.

Does this pose a real threat to our free will? Is the idea that 'my genes made me do it' any more troubling than the idea that 'my brain made me do it'? To answer this question, we first need to get clear on just what the research about heritability does and doesn't show.

Tim Spector has been studying identical twins at King's College London for over twenty years. When I met him at his office in St Thomas' Hospital, he gave measured, cautious and qualified answers to all my questions about the importance of genes in determining who we are. It would have been a very different conversation if I had spoken to him during what he now sees as his 'overzealous genetic phase'.

From the start of his research, it became evident to Spector that identical twins were always more similar than brothers or sisters or non-identical twins. At the time, however, 'social scientists hated the idea' that genes were an important determinant of who we were, 'particularly in those rather controversial areas like IQ, personality and beliefs'. His zeal was in part 'a reaction to all those people saying there's absolutely no way these things are genetic'. As 'one of the many scientists who took the gene-centric view of the universe for granted', he wanted 'to prove them wrong, and to prove that there's nothing that's not genetic to some extent'. As he recalls in his book *Identically Different*, he spent 'seventeen years producing hundreds of twin studies trying to convince a sceptical public and scientific world that virtually every trait and disease had a major genetic influence'.[1]

It is perhaps understandable that Spector got caught up in gene mania. The launch in 1990 of the Human Genome Project to map the complete sequence of human DNA started a decade that would mark the high point of optimism about how much our genes could tell us. Daniel Koshland, then editor of *Science*, one of the most prestigious journals in the world, captured the zeitgeist when he wrote: 'The benefits to science of the genome project are clear. Illnesses such as manic depression, Alzheimer's, schizophrenia, and heart disease are probably all multigenic and even more difficult to unravel than cystic fibrosis. Yet these diseases are at the root of many current societal problems.'[2] Genes would help us uncover the secrets of all kinds of ills, from the psychological to the physical.

Ten years later, the then president of the United States and the British Prime Minister were among the guests gathered to 'celebrate the revelation of the first draft of the human book of life', as Francis Collins, the director of the Human Genome Project, put it.[3] 'We try to be cautious on days like this,' said the ABC news anchor, 'but this map marks the beginning of an era of discovery that will affect the lives of every human being, with implications for science, history, business, ethics, religion, and, of course, medicine.'

By that time, genes were no longer simply the key to understanding health: they had become the skeleton key for unlocking almost all the mysteries of human existence. For almost every aspect of life – criminality, fidelity, political persuasion, religious belief – someone would claim to find a gene for it. In 2005 in the US, Stephen Mobley even tried to avoid execution by claiming that his murder of a pizza store manager was the result of a mutation in the monoamine oxidase A (MAOA) gene. The judge turned down the appeal, saying that the law was not ready to accept such evidence.[4] The basic idea, however, that the low-MAOA gene is a major contributing cause of violence has become widely accepted, and it is now commonly called the 'warrior gene'.

Among scientists, faith in the explanatory power of genes has waned in recent years. Back in the 1990s, the geneticist Steve Jones found that 'Those interested in the genetics of human behaviour do not themselves suffer from undue modesty.' But he could already see this was misplaced. 'There have been announcements of the discovery of single genes for manic depression, schizophrenia and alcoholism. All have been withdrawn.'[5]

Today, few scientists would now say that it is 'the gene for violence'. In fact, when it comes to almost everything about human beings, especially personality traits and belief, it is generally agreed that there is no simple 'gene for' anything. Almost all inherited features or traits are the products of complex interactions of numerous genes. However, the fact that there is no one genetic trigger has not by itself undermined the claim that many of our deepest character traits, dispositions and even opinions are genetically determined.

This worry is only slightly tempered by the recent growth of epigenetics, which shows how many inherited traits only get 'switched on' in certain environments. The reason this doesn't remove all fears is that most of this switching on and off occurs either in utero or in early childhood. The worry that 'my genes made me do it' is not removed by finding out that those genes were set later than at conception.

What might reduce our alarm, however, is an understanding of what genetic studies really show. The key concept here is of heritability. We are often told that many traits are highly heritable: IQ is around 70 per cent heritable, spirituality 40 to 50 per cent and happiness around 50 per cent. These figures sound very high. But they do not mean what they appear to mean to the statistically untrained eye.

Take rheumatoid arthritis, which is 60 to 70 per cent heritable. Spector found that 'of identical twins with the disease, eighty-five per cent of sisters never got it, even with similar lifestyles'. The same pattern was true for most diseases he studied: 'there was rarely more than a fifty per cent chance of both twins getting the same disease, and usually the figure was much lower'.

How can this be true if conditions are 60 per cent or more heritable? The common mistake people make is to assume that if, for example, autism is 90 per cent heritable, then 90 per cent of autistic people got the condition from their parents. But 'it's nothing about chance or risk of passing it on', says Spector. 'All journalists get it wrong. We did something on infidelity – fifty per cent heritable – and they said if your parents have strayed you have a fifty per cent chance of straying yourself, and that's not true.'

So if heritability doesn't mean the chance of passing something on, what does it mean? 'It simply means how much of the variation within a given population is down to genes,' says Spector. Crucially, this will be different according to the environment of that population.

A clear example is smoking and lung cancer. We know that smoking is the prime cause of lung cancer. So what would happen if everyone smoked twenty cigarettes a day? In such a world, everyone would be exposed to exactly the same amount of the carcinogens. But not all of them would get lung cancer. So what would make the difference between those who did and those who didn't? Genetic predisposition. In this world lung cancer would be almost 100 per cent heritable: the only thing that would explain the difference between those who got lung cancer and those who didn't would be their genes. This is true even though the causes of lung cancer are almost entirely environmental.

Another neat example is height, which is 90 per cent heritable. But as Spector points out, 'the Dutch have grown six inches in fifty years', and 'you can't change your genes in fifty years'. Genes are a good predictor of whether you will be taller or shorter than your peers, but they are no good at all at predicting how tall you will be, unless you know how conducive to healthy growth your environment is.

Heritability therefore tells us nothing about your chances of inheriting a trait, and it differs depending on the environment. Spector spells out what this means with something like IQ, which has a heritability of 70 per cent on average. 'If you go to the US, around Harvard, it's above ninety per cent,' he says. Why? Because people selected to go there tend to come from middle-class families who have all offered their children similar, excellent educational opportunities. Having all been given very similar upbringings, almost all the remaining variation is down to genes. In contrast, 'if you go to Detroit suburbs, crack, single mums, it's close to zero per cent', because the wretched environment is having such a strong effect. In general, Spector believes that 'Any change in environment has a much greater effect on IQ than genes,' as it does on almost every human characteristic. That's why if you want to predict whether someone believes in God, it's more useful to know that they live in Texas than what their genes are.

Statistical illiteracy is not the only reason why the importance of environmental factors is so often drowned out. We tend to be mesmerised by the similarities between identical twins and notice the differences much less. I was surprised to discover that even identical twins such as Dan and Scott do this. One of them (I find it hard to distinguish) told me that 'I had a set of identical twins at my school and I thought it was the weirdest thing. I couldn't tell them apart and I was fascinated by them in the same way that I realised people were fascinated by us.' I met Dan and Scott at a twins event at the Science Museum in London, and they told me that the first time they went to such a gathering, 'We were just walking around thinking, "This is really weird!"', an experience the identical twins Margaret and Helen laughed along with in recognition. Even those researching genetics sometimes play on this to get attention for their work. All the twins at the museum, for instance, were asked to dress identically for the event, which Dan/Scott was 'not very comfortable doing'.

But it could be that the uncanniness is drawing our attention to all the wrong things. 'When you look at twins,' says Spector, 'the one thing that always seems to come out are the subconscious tics, mannerisms, postures, the way they laugh. They sit the same, cross their legs the same, pick up cups of coffee the same, even if they hate each other or they've been separated all their lives.' It's as though we cannot help thinking that such things reflect deeper similarities even though they are actually the most superficial features to compare. Spector agrees with this suggestion, saying, 'We put much more importance on these things than we should.' For example, although I can't tell them apart, Margaret and Helen are very different in all sorts of ways: one is academic, the other practical; one bisexual, the other heterosexual; one a union activist, the other a Liberal Democrat activist.

There is also a potential reporting bias in some of the more incredible stories of twin similarities, such as the two Jims. Spector points out that the twins who took part in the Minnesota study answered thousands of questions. Given the relative frequency in populations of common names and the popularity of certain brands, chance alone would predict that every now and again such surveys would reveal twins marrying people with the same name, or preferring the same beer.

As I discovered, if you can stop yourself staring at the similarities between twins, literally and metaphorically, and listen properly to their stories, you can see how their differences are at least as telling as their similarities.

Twins were the last thing a 1940s working-class family with five children in Powys, Mid Wales needed. So, identical or not, the two girls were packed off to different aunts. After three months, Judy returned to her biological mother, her aunt having enough on her plate with her own kids. But for the childless fifty-year-old couple who took on Ann (without ever formally adopting her), the late opportunity for parenthood was a blessing and she stayed.

Although the girls grew up in the same town, they lived in different areas and went to different schools. They were discouraged from seeing each other, perhaps due to Ann's aunt and uncle's fear that if a bond grew she would return to her birth mother. The girls went to the same Sunday School for a while, but it wasn't a place for talking or playing, and so they remained strangers.

The two households were very different. Judy's father drove trains inside the steelworks, and her mother never worked, like most women at the time. They lived in a basic two-up, two-down house with a toilet at the bottom of the garden. Her four older brothers were all out working by the time she was five and, left with her older sister Yvonne, Judy says, 'I was the boss, even though I was the youngest.'

Ann was brought up in a 1939 semi-detached house, very nice for its time, with a toilet indoors as well as out the back. Her father was also a manual labourer in the steelworks, but they were relatively well off, partly because they hadn't had children but also because they were 'very careful with money'. The rest of the family used to say her mother 'would skin a flea for ha'penny'. Ann recalls that 'the sugar bowl was never filled so as not to encourage people to take too much. They weren't mean with their time but they were mean with their money.' She describes them as 'Victorians', their austere values reflected in the fact that her mother 'never wore lipstick or a bra'.

The two sisters are telling me this in Ann's home in Crickhowell on the edge of the Brecon Beacons, over coffee and home-made Welsh cakes. Whereas Ann remembers that 'All the time in the world was given to me,' Judy tells me she 'was a street kid, always out. I never sat on a chair until I was thirteen. I went to the gym a lot and we would climb trees and things like that. I was a right little tomboy.'

'I would be reading,' says Ann. 'That was probably the difference. I always had my nose in a book because I was on my own.'

'I can't remember reading a book before I was eleven,' says Judy, whose family didn't have books in the house, 'just one for Christmas.' That was until Judy's father bought a set of encyclopedias, as Ann reminded her.

'Number five was famous people and that was the only one I ever read,' says Judy. 'I never wanted them.'

'I would have loved them!' replies Ann.

Add to that the fact that, as Ann says, 'I went to a good school and Judy went to not a good school because of the areas we were brought up in,' it perhaps came as no surprise that whereas Ann passed the eleven-plus examination and so got into the grammar school, Judy didn't, and ended up at the secondary modern. No surprise, that is, except to Judy herself.

'I was shocked when I failed the eleven-plus because I was one of the brightest in the class and I knew I was one of the brightest,' she says, her voice still full of outrage. Then, as now, having books at home, involved parents and a school that encouraged you to aspire made more of a difference to educational outcomes than the raw IQ bequeathed to you by your genes.

Judy did get a second chance. At her school, they only taught arithmetic, not geometry or algebra. But when she took the Monmouthshire Certificate of Education at age fifteen, she got 100 per cent in arithmetic. 'Somebody somewhere saw this and thought, bloomin' heck, what's going on here?' she recalls. 'So they offered me a place at the grammar school.'

When she got there she was doing algebra and geometry in a class where everyone else had already being doing it for three years.

Unsurprisingly she struggled, not helped by a 'horrible maths teacher who thought the world of Ann, and who said to me, "You're not like your sister".' They say talent will out, but when social structures are against you, talent soon retreats again. After four months, Judy quit and went to work in a furniture shop.

Ann, meanwhile, breezed through school and left at sixteen because her now sixty-six-year-old father was retiring and 'I just felt that it wasn't fair for me to stay on at school when they were on a pension'. Despite her parents wanting her to continue her education, she left and got a job in the council offices. The sisters' paths were diverging, Ann's taking her to white-collar work and Judy to the shop floor. Judy did aspire to more and went to Bath to train as a nurse, even though she now finds the idea hilarious. 'I was never going to be a nurse in a million years!' Six months into her training, she got pregnant, and so returned home and got married.

This is the point of the story for the obligatory uncanny-twin-parallel moment. Ann also got pregnant, two months earlier than Judy, and quit her job. Not only that, but both fathers, soon husbands, turned out to be very violent.

However, the differences are more instructive than what may just be coincidences. Ann didn't stay married for long. 'I left and went back home, and they were very supportive when they found out what was going on.' Judy, in contrast, stood by her man for seventeen years. 'I did leave him, mind, but I kept going back', because she 'didn't have the support. I had three children by the time I was twenty-one. I would go to my mother's but then she'd go on about the price of bread. She was such a caring woman,' she says with deadpan irony. 'My mother's attitude was, you made your bed, you lie on it.'

Ann understands Judy's acquiescence perfectly. 'Imagine being at home, with two children, no qualifications, nothing on the horizon to see your life was going to get better, which I did have.'

Ann went back to her studies and trained as a teacher. In time she would do a degree in maths with the Open University. 'I ended up as the deputy head of the primary school here, and I loved it,' she says.

In her late twenties, Judy finally got her chance to shine academically. She was working in a greengrocer's shop when somebody told her about TOPS (Training Opportunities Scheme), which Judy was amazed to discover 'actually paid you to go to college'. Despite being told all the places were taken, her determination and persistence got her in. The course ended with thirteen exams, including four O levels, and she passed every one. 'That's when things started to change for me. And that's also when I started realising these beatings weren't really my fault. So I left him then.' First, she worked in a solicitor's office, where she learnt about how to get a divorce. Then she worked in the civil service for thirty years, saying, 'I enjoyed it, absolutely loved it.'

The two only really started a proper sibling relationship after Ann read about the Minnesota research in the paper and wrote to the university about her and her sister. When they were forty-eight, they travelled together to the US. Now the twins are both retired. Judy says, 'I think from where we started we've travelled the same distance.'

But there were important differences in how their lives went, and so too in the people they became. Most obviously, Ann has always had more money, but you can also see the effects of their different backgrounds on their health. 'Judy's had a hysterectomy, I haven't,' says Ann. 'Judy's got a problem with her kidneys. I don't. Judy's got blood pressure, I haven't. But she's stronger than me.'

'Plus I've got a load of stamina,' adds Judy, 'because I can keep my hand in cold water for much longer.' She also says that she's had false teeth since she was thirty-two, unlike Ann. Judy smoked for many years, whereas Ann never did. That might explain why, in

Minnesota, Judy managed six minutes on the treadmill and was exhausted, while Ann did twelve and could have gone on.

There are also differences in how they think and behave socially. Although their political views are very similar, Judy says, 'I'm a Christian, well, probably agnostic, I think,' whereas Ann is 'a confirmed atheist'. Ann also thinks she's 'much more diplomatic. Judy is just rude. That's probably the educational background coming through. "Interfering" is too strong a word, but Judy is more involved with her children and grandchildren in an advisory capacity, whereas I wouldn't do that.'

'Ann is far more gullible,' adds Judy. 'She's not as streetwise.' Ann agrees. 'With adults I always believe that people will tell the truth.'

'I'm far more judgemental,' says Judy.

'Much more black and white,' agrees Ann.

'Down the middle. If it's wrong, it's wrong.' Much of this, they agree, is surely down to culture, with Ann being encouraged to adopt more genteel middle-class ways and Judy following the blunter conventions of the working classes. This is also reflected in what they say they would order if we were in a pub right now.

'I drink vodka,' says Judy.

'I drink wine, or gin and tonic,' says Ann.

Ann and Judy's story is a valuable corrective for anyone who has been too impressed by tales of how identical twins show that we are basically nothing but the products of our genes. Of course the women are similar in many respects, but sitting opposite them on the sofa, it is as obvious to me as to anyone else that they are two very different people in important ways. Our genes set down what might be described as a field of possibilities. These set limits on what we are to become, so whatever our upbringings, most of us will tend towards introversion or extroversion, jollity or sobriety, facility with words or numbers. But this is far from the claim that all we become is essentially written in our genes. Rather, various options are pencilled in, and it is our environments which determine which get inked.

Genetic research is quite new and has understandably grabbed the headlines over recent decades. But as the field develops, all informed minds accept that in the nature versus nurture debate, there is no winner. Both have their role to play in shaping who we are. That, however, does nothing to calm the fundamental challenge genetics poses to free will. For consider what the nurture side of this discussion has to say about who we are. A person's religious conviction, for example, is often considered to be a core part of their identity. And yet as Bertrand Russell pointed out, 'with very few exceptions, the religion which a man accepts is that of the community in which he lives, which makes it obvious that the influence of environment is what has led him to accept the religion in question'.[6] Even the exceptions prove the rule. There are some Anglo-Saxon British converts to Islam, for example, but there certainly weren't any before Islam established itself as a large minority religion in the United Kingdom. Religious belief is largely inherited, not through genes, but by socialisation through parents.

All manner of moral beliefs are also quite clearly the product of the culture you live in. Disgust at eating dogs is normal in Kent, rare in Korea. Similarly, personality traits are affected by where you grow up, with Americans generally being more demonstrative than Britons. Political affiliation also has a strong socially determined dimension. You are far more likely to become a Conservative if you grew up in affluent, rural Surrey than if you were brought up in the tenements of inner-city Glasgow.

The issue of free will does not depend on how you resolve the nature versus nurture debate. The problem is that who we are appears to be a product of *both* nature and nurture, in whatever proportion they contribute, *and nothing else.* In accounting for who we are, nature + nurture = 100 per cent. You are shaped by forces beyond yourself, and do not choose what you become. And so when you go on to make the choices in life that really matter, you do so on the basis of beliefs, values and dispositions that you did not choose. In that sense, your choice is not fundamentally free because you could not have become other than the person you are.

Although this may appear troubling, it is hard to see how it could be any other way. For example, say you support a more redistributive tax system, because you think that is fair. Where did that sense of fairness come from? You may well have thought it through and come to a conclusion. But what did you bring to that process? A combination of abilities and dispositions that you were born with, and information and thinking skills that you acquired. In other words, a combination of hereditary factors and environment. There is no third place for anything else to come from. You are not responsible for how you emerged from the womb, nor for the world you found yourself in. Once you became old enough and sufficiently self-aware to think for yourself, the key determinants in your personality and outlook were already set. Yes, your views might be changed later in life by powerful experiences or persuasive books. But again, you do not choose for these things to change you. The very way we speak about such experiences suggests this. 'This book changed my life,' we say, not 'I changed my life with this book', acknowledging that having read it, we did not choose to be different; we simply could never be the same again.

The literature on free will tends to focus on moments of choice: was I free at that point to do other than what I did? When we ask this, it often seems to us that only one option was viable. Sometimes this is because we think circumstances constrain us. But perhaps a more fundamental reason why at the moment of choice we cannot do otherwise is that we cannot be other than who we are, and so the idea that we are radically free to do anything at all makes no sense.

The nature of the chooser is the key determinant at the moment of choice: *who we are* comes first and *what we do* follows.

This would appear to take us closer to what really seems to matter to people when they consider their freedom. The strongest defence of an action is that being the person you are with your values and beliefs, you could not have done anything else. That is why when people are asked to justify why they made the choices they did, they often appeal to their desires and values. For example, E. M. Forster once wrote: 'If I had to choose between betraying my country and betraying my friend, I hope I should have the guts to betray my country.' The reason for this is that he valued friendship over 'the idea of causes', which he claimed to 'hate'.[7]

To be considered truly free, then, it would seem to be necessary for us to be in some sense responsible for being the people we are, and that responsibility needs to go 'all the way down': it has to be down to you and you alone what values and beliefs you hold dear and act upon. If we are not responsible for who we are, how can we be held responsible for what we do? If someone is not responsible for valuing their religion more than their country, how can we blame them if they commit a criminal act that expresses this fundamental commitment? But when we consider the dual roles of nature and nurture, the values we hold and beliefs we assert do not appear to be a matter of choice. We are formed by forces ultimately beyond our control. This thought, once made explicit, leads many to the conclusion that free will and responsibility are impossible. If you dig deep enough into what made us who we are, eventually (although usually not after that long) you come across some key formative factors that we did not control. And if they are beyond our control, how can we be responsible for them?

On reflection, though, we ought to be more sanguine about our lack of complete control. The first step towards acceptance is to realise that it would be a very odd person whose actions did not in some sense flow from her values and beliefs. And yet the more strongly we hold these, the less we really feel free to choose other than the way we do. In 1521, the Reformation priest Martin Luther, for example, is reported to have told his accusers at the Diet of Worms, 'Here I stand. I can do no other.' His convictions were so deep that it was not possible for him to do other than what he did. This is not a denial of his freedom but an assertion of his freedom to act according to his values.

No sane person would want the ability to choose anything at all. If you are appalled by needless violence, you want it to be true that you would recoil from torture, not that you would be as free to do it as to not do it. The power to choose just anything is not a freedom worth wanting. The person who believes he could equally well have rejected or accepted a life partner clearly doesn't have the strength of conviction necessary to make the choice. We want many of our choices to flow with a kind of necessity from our beliefs and values.

We cannot change our characters on a whim, and we would not want it any other way. A Christian does not want the freedom to wake up one day and become a Muslim. A committed family man does not want to find it as easy to run off with the au pair as to stick with his children and their mother. A fan of Shostakovich does not, usually at least, wish she could just decide to prefer Andrew Lloyd Webber.

The critical point is that these key commitments don't strike us primarily as choices. You like the things you do because you think they are great. You live with the person you do because you love her. You support a political cause because you think it is just. You don't choose what you think is great, who you should love, or what is just. To think of these fundamental life commitments as choices is rather peculiar, perhaps a distortion created by the contemporary emphasis on choice as being at the heart of freedom.

What's more, the idea that any kind of rational creature could choose its own basic dispositions and values is incoherent. For on what basis could such a choice be made? Without any values or dispositions, one would have no reason to prefer some over others. Imagine the anteroom in heaven, where people wait to be prepared for life on earth. Some angel asks you, would you like to be a Republican or a Democrat? How could you answer if you did not already have some commitments and values that would tip the balance either side? It would be impossible.

Throughout human history, people have had no problem with the idea that their basic personality types were there from birth. Many people, perhaps the majority, believe that time of birth determines character, as evidenced by the enduring appeal of horoscopes. The idea of taking after your parents is an almost universal cultural constant. Discovering just how much nature and nurture contribute to who we are is interesting, but doesn't change the fact that traits are not chosen, and that no one ever thought they were.

The extent to which beliefs and values flow from personality and character traits is perhaps not so easily acknowledged. We're happy to think we might be born outgoing, for example, but less sanguine about the fact that our political commitments are at least in part based on our temperament and upbringing. But accepting this is ultimately more honest and liberating than denying it. Recognising how much our beliefs and commitments are shaped by factors beyond our control actually helps us to gain more control of them. It allows us to question our sense that something is obviously true by provoking us to ask whether it would appear so obvious if our upbringing or character had been different. It is only by recognising how much is not in our power that we can seize control of that which is. Perhaps most importantly, accepting how much belief is the product of an unchosen past should help us to be less dogmatic and more understanding of others. It doesn't mean anything goes, of course, or that no view is right or wrong. But it does mean that no one is able to be perfectly objective, and so we should humbly accept that although objective truth is worth striving for, none of us could claim to have fully attained it.

Some may not be convinced yet that we should be so relaxed about our debt to nature and nurture. Unless the buck stops with us, it seems to many unjust to hold people responsible for their actions. The philosopher Galen Strawson argues that this 'is obvious in such a way that insisting on it too much is likely to make it seem less obvious than it is'. At the risk of introducing less clarity than is needed, he nonetheless formalises the reasoning behind the thought into what he calls 'The Basic Argument'. (1) Nothing can be *causa sui* – nothing can be the cause of itself. (2) In order to be truly morally responsible for one's actions one would have to be *causa sui*, at least in certain crucial mental respects. (3) Therefore nothing can be truly morally responsible. It follows from this that 'It is exactly as just to punish people or reward people for their actions as it is to punish or reward them for the (natural) colour of their hair or the (natural) shape of their faces.'[8]

Given that the idea of being the *causa sui* is 'the best self-contradiction hitherto imagined', as Nietzsche put it, this argument strikes many people as unanswerable.[9] It is only obviously correct, however, if we assume that the sole variety of real responsibility is *ultimate* responsibility. This 'condition of ultimate responsibility' is defined by Robert Kane as: 'To be ultimately responsible for an action, an agent must be responsible for anything that is a sufficient cause or motive for the action's occurring.'[10] That's a pretty tough condition to meet, and it is certainly not one that we would insist on when using our everyday notion of responsibility.

This is most evident in cases of negligence. Imagine you postpone maintaining a roof properly and it collapses during an exceptionally fierce storm, killing or injuring people below. The roof would not *ultimate responsibility*

have collapsed if there had not been a storm, and the weather is clearly not in your control. But that does not mean you should not be held responsible for failing to maintain the building properly.

If the only real responsibility were ultimate responsibility, then there could never be any responsibility at all, because everything that happens involves factors both within and outside of our control. As John Martin Fischer succinctly and accurately puts it, 'Total control is a total fantasy – metaphysical megalomania.'[11] And why would we think that only this kind of responsibility counts? As Daniel Dennett said of Galen Strawson, 'he's defined ultimate responsibility in such a way that it's impossible. OK, how about *almost* ultimate responsibility? What's wrong with that?'

Many arguments that purport to debunk free will are powerful only if you buy into the often unstated premise that real responsibility is ultimate responsibility. Saul Smilansky at least has the decency to make this assumption explicit. In what I take to be the ultimate example of the fixation on the ultimate, he writes, 'if there is no libertarian free will, no one can be ultimately in control, ultimately responsible, for this self and its determinations. *Everything* that takes place on the compatibilist level becomes on the ultimate hard determinist level "what was merely *there*", ultimately deriving from causes beyond the control of the participants.'[12] I couldn't agree more, but read it again, removing all the 'ultimates', and the case weakens to the point of collapse.

Almost all those who deny free will define responsibility as though it must be total and absolute, or it is nothing at all. The Dutch neuroscientist Dick Swaab, who calls free will 'an illusion', does so by endorsing the definition of free will by Joseph L. Price (a scientist, not a philosopher) as 'the ability to choose to act or refrain from action without extrinsic or intrinsic constraints'. No wonder he is forced to conclude that 'Our current knowledge of neurobiology makes it clear that there is no such thing as absolute freedom.' Similarly, he claims that the existence of unconscious deci-sion-making in the brain leaves 'no room for a purely conscious, free will'.[13] That's true. The only question is why one would believe such *absolute* or *pure* freedom is possible or necessary.

The answer to this might lie in the development of Christian thought. Although it is often assumed that the notion of free will as uncaused action and thought is simply a common sense one, it is not found universally, geographically or historically. Perhaps, instead, it is an artefact of western culture. An invaluable source here is the late scholar of ancient philosophy Michael Frede, whose study of the origins of the idea of free will in classical thought provides a much-needed context for contemporary discussions.

Frede makes a compelling case that the ancients understood responsibility and voluntary action without anything like the con-temporary idea of free will. 'We should carefully distinguish between the belief in a free will and the ordinary belief that at least sometimes we are responsible for what we are doing, because we are not forced or made to behave in this way but really want or even choose or decide to act in this way,' he writes. He cites Aristotle as 'a good example of a philosopher who is committed to the ordinary belief but doesn't resort to the notion of a free will to account for this belief'.[14]

It does not straightforwardly follow from this that our notion of free will just didn't exist in ancient Greece. As the Christian philoso-pher Timothy O'Connor put it to me, 'A notion can be implicit in thinking without its necessarily being made a focal point of theo-retical discussion.' That's true, but it is also very easy to assume that a notion we find so natural and familiar is lurking unstated in the background when in fact we have placed it there ourselves. There is also the question of why otherwise perfectly articulate and care-ful philosophers would not have brought the notion to the surface, if it really was so fundamental. At the end of the day, it is very hard to show conclusively that an idea is or is not 'implicit' in a discourse that only now exists as an historical record. Whichever way you look at it, though, the Greek discussion of free will shows that our contemporary notion is not needed to make sense of it.

Frede suggests that, in explaining the absence of the idea of free will, 'Perhaps the most crucial difference is that nobody in antiquity had the notion of laws of nature, meaning a body of laws which govern and explain the behaviour of all objects, irrespective of their kind.'[15] We might think that shows a deficiency in their thinking that we have got beyond: just because the Greeks got on perfectly well without a notion of free will, it doesn't mean they were right to do so. The point is, however, that their conceptions of responsibility did not rest on any assumptions about the laws of nature or their absence. Such notions were simply irrelevant.

Frede claims that we have to wait until the third quarter of the second century AD to find the first person ever to use the expression 'the freedom of the will' (*eleutheria tēs prohaireseōs*). This rarely heralded thinker was Tatian, who in his *Oratio ad Graecos* argued that the idea of free will was required 'in order that the bad man may be justly punished'. The passage in question is worth quoting in full because it suggests why the notion needed to be invented:

> For the heavenly Logos, a spirit emanating from the Father and a Logos from the Logos-power, in imitation of the Father who begat Him made man an image of immortality, so that, as incorruption is with God, in like manner, man, sharing in a part of God, might have the immortal principle also. The Logos, too, before the creation of men, was the Framer of angels. And each of these two orders of creatures was made free to act as it pleased, not having the nature of good, which again is with God alone, but is brought to perfection in men through their freedom of choice, in order that the bad man may be justly

punished, having become depraved through his own fault, but the just man be deservedly praised for his virtuous deeds, since in the exercise of his free choice he refrained from transgressing the will of God.[16]

Ordinary punishment, praise or blame may not require ultimate responsibility, merely some sense of being sufficiently in control of your actions or responsive to reasons and incentives. Eternal damnation, on the other hand, is a very different thing. If your wickedness is not *entirely* your fault, how could we justify punishment without end? As Augustine would put it a few centuries later, 'The very fact that anyone who uses free will to sin is divinely punished shows that free will was given to enable human beings to live rightly, for such punishment would be unjust if free will had been given both for living rightly and for sinning.'[17]

According to Frede, there is a second theological reason why Origen, Augustine and many who followed them needed the idea of free will. To put it bluntly, if the buck doesn't stop with us, then it can only stop with the one who created us. But that would mean that God was ultimately responsible for our wickedness. If we are bad, and God made us, then God created our badness. So it was necessary to attribute 'to human beings themselves the difficulties they find themselves in as a result of their own choice and doing'.[18]

Of course, religion is as diverse as philosophy and there are examples of theologians who have denied free will, most notably Martin Luther and John Calvin, both important figures in the sixteenth-century Protestant Reformation. For them, salvation is a gift of God's grace and it is impious vanity to believe that human beings can achieve it by their own free actions. As Luther wrote, 'For the reason why grace is needed, and why the help of grace is given, is that free choice by itself can do nothing.'[19] However, this is very much the minority view, one which is very hard to square with the justice of God punishing people for what they do through no will of their own. Hence most monotheists agree with Erasmus that free will is theologically necessary 'to allow the ungodly, who have deliberately fallen short of the grace of God, to be deservedly condemned; to clear God of the false accusation of cruelty and injustice; to free us from despair, protect us from complacency, and spur us on to moral endeavour'.[20]

This did present a challenge for theologians, however, since the concept of free will appears to be as absent in scripture as it was in ancient philosophy. Frede argues that when Origen, 'the first Christian author ever to write in detail and systematically about the free will', collected Bible verses supporting the existence of free will, 'all he can find are passages which you might take to imply that there is a free will but only if you already believe that there is such a thing'.[21] Indeed, some scripture seems to explicitly rule out free will. Philippians 2 v.13 says: 'For it is God which worketh in you both to will and to do of his good pleasure.'

The idea that ultimate responsibility is required for any meaningful form of free will is one of the biggest red herrings in the history of the debate. Ultimate responsibility is only needed to justify ultimate punishment. However, as many have argued, ultimate responsibility cannot exist, which is perhaps the most convincing argument against the very possibility of eternal damnation by a benevolent God. The only forms of freedom and responsibility that are both possible and worth having are those that are partial, not absolute. This is an idea we will be returning to later when we consider the criminal justice system.

The major challenges to the idea of free will that have emerged from recent science turn out not to rest very much on new developments after all. They simply build on older worries, ones which arose as soon as some of our ancient Greek forebears realised that human beings were fully part of nature. These worries rest on four assumptions which we have examined in the last two chapters and found to be questionable: that a free choice must not be determined or even too conditioned by its past causes; that free choice has to be entirely the result of a conscious decision; that to choose freely it must always have been possible that you could have done otherwise; and that to be free requires being ultimately responsible for being the person you are.

There is perhaps one broader assumption, which underpins all four. That is, that freedom requires a complete absence of constraint on what we do. Anything that limits the possible choices we could make is a limit on freedom. Freedom requires being equally able to take any of the options available.

But choice is only ever meaningful within restraints. Free will has to be some kind of mean between two extremes. At one extreme, we have the character of the human butterfly, whose choices emerge from nowhere, with no causes and which have no pattern. She declares undying love to one man one minute and then tries to kill him the next. This is not freedom but a random sequence of actions. At the other extreme we have the strict determinism of the Terminator, a science-fiction cyborg sent by its creators to 'kill John Connor' and unable to reflect on or revise this objective. Freedom must fall somewhere between these: either acting without any limits or acting under rigid constraint.

That is the kind of free will we need to look for. If we become accustomed to thinking of freedom as completely unfettered, anything more limited will at first sight look like an emaciated form of liberty. You might even dismiss it as mere wiggle room: the ability to make limited choices within a framework of great restraint. But that would be a mistake. Unfettered freedom is not only an illusion; it makes no sense. It would not be desirable even if we could have it. Choices are not meaningful unless they reflect values, and values cannot be meaningfully chosen unless you already have some.

The scientific world view, therefore, destroys only a straw-man version of free will, a naive conception that would crumble under rational scrutiny long before scientists could get their hands on it. Quite simply, the commonplace idea of free will we have lost was always wrong. Good riddance to it. Now it is time to find a form of freedom really worth having.

PART THREE

Freedom Regained

4

The Artist

O n one of the walls of Jamaica Street studios in Bristol, someone has painted a quote by the sculptor and installation artist
Cornelia Parker: 'There's such a freedom about being an artist.'
Clearly the idea resonates with many of the three dozen or so people
who create their work in the studios. It also resonates more widely.
Creative expression is one of the paradigms of human freedom. Yet
strangely enough, when discussing freedom, scientists and philosophers usually talk instead about people's choice of hot beverage, or
decisions to press buttons in laboratories. If we really want to know
about the kind of freedom that matters to us, wouldn't we do better
to look at artists?

To try to understand better how artists might provide a positive
paradigm of freedom, I met Grayson Perry, whose now famous pots
won him the Turner Prize in 2003. When I started by asking him
an open question about what freedom meant to him, his first reaction was entirely negative.

'In the modern context the word freedom slightly makes me
cringe,' he said, 'because it implies internet-provoked rebellion that
doesn't really know where it's going. There's this idea of freedom
now which is easily evoked which is kind of like, we want to do

what we want, whatever that is, though we're not quite sure. Freedom is this abstract thing that just leads either to a tyranny of choice or giving up the free will to comply to any tradition or norm, which might actually be quite good for you. Rules are there for a reason and there seem to be a lot of babies thrown out with bathwater when it comes to freedom.'

Perry put his finger on several key points here, the most general being that if we think of freedom only in its most typical, contemporary sense, it is not something to be coveted or treasured. Freedom merely as absence of constraint and presence of consumer choice is a very thin value indeed, and it's no wonder Perry has little time for it. These opening remarks by Perry were an early indication of how much the artist's conception of freedom runs counter to the freedom of received and academic wisdom.

The most striking difference between textbook freedom and artistic freedom is that artists often report a frequent absence of conscious control. For example, the writer Diana Athill wrote, 'In the early 1960s nine stories "happened" to me. I say "happened" because I did not decide to write them, but suddenly felt a peculiar sort of itch, which produced them.'[1]

This way of thinking is typical of writers and other kinds of artist. Talking about composing the soundtrack for the film *Chariots of Fire*, Vangelis said, 'My main inspiration was the story itself. The rest I did instinctively, without thinking about anything else, other than to express my feelings with the technological means available to me at the time.'[2] Similarly, Bruce Watson of the rock band Big Country told me that when he is writing a song, 'I never push for it. It finds you, doesn't it? You never try to force it, you just let it happen naturally.'

Indeed, some go so far as to say that even attempting to impose too much conscious control is counterproductive, and that it is vital to let ideas simply come. 'To try to know beforehand is to freeze and kill,' wrote Ray Bradbury in one of his essays about creativity. 'Self-consciousness is the enemy of all art.'[3]

Bradbury is a particularly lucid articulator of these matters. Remember, for example, how some neuroscientists claim that the conscious mind often being the last to know what we decide is a threat to human freedom? Bradbury reports just this kind of experience, but with delight rather than alarm. Long after writing *Fahrenheit 451*, his dystopian novel about a world where books are banned, he realised that his central character, Montag, was named after a paper manufacturer, while another, Faber, a maker of pencils. (He had not yet realised that Faber is also a major literary publisher.) 'What a sly thing my subconscious was to name them thus,' he remarks. 'And not to tell *me*!'

Of course, artists do often exercise conscious control. But on such occasions they tend if anything to feel less rather than more free than when on autopilot. Being aware of the multiplicity of choices and having to decide between them feels like a problem; just knowing what you want to do next is the solution.

Perhaps the worst place for any artist to be is alone with her conscious mind. Writer's block obstructs the usually easy flow of ideas, which come without the mediation of conscious thought. When writers hit such blocks, their conscious minds are often too much to the fore, which leaves them with the blank page. 'Your unconscious can't work when you are breathing down its neck,' as the novelist Anne Lamott put it. 'You'll sit there going, "Are you done in there yet, are you done in there yet?" But it is trying to tell you nicely, "Shut up and go away."'[4] Similarly, Hemingway warned that 'if you think about [writing] consciously or worry about it you will kill it and your brain will be tired before you start'.[5]

Perry does not have much truck with the stereotype of artistic creation as a kind of pure, spontaneous outpouring, exemplified by the Jackson Pollock-like character in Martin Scorsese's film *Life*

Lessons, who creates huge canvases in passionate frenzies, accompanied by a driving rock soundtrack.[6] 'The idea that you'll know when this amazing breakthrough will happen I think is a romantic myth. It's incremental often, creativity, not revelatory It's not like Archimedes in the bath.'

[handwritten margin note: Eureka Moment]

Evidence that this kind of revelation is not the norm is provided by the exceptionality of Coleridge's experience of writing 'Kubla Khan'. In the preface to that poem, Coleridge describes himself in the third person falling into an opium-induced sleep,

> at least of the external senses, during which time he has the most vivid confidence, that he could not have composed less than from two to three hundred lines; if that indeed can be called composition in which all the images rose up before him as things, with a parallel production of the correspondent expressions, without any sensation or consciousness of effort. On awakening he appeared to himself to have a distinct recollection of the whole, and taking his pen, ink, and paper, instantly and eagerly wrote down the lines that are here preserved.

The bathetic coda to this is that he was interrupted by a man on some business from Porlock and couldn't complete the task.

[handwritten margin note: redrafting]

We do not know if the process was as seamless as Coleridge describes, but it would not have become such a distinctive, unique moment in the history of English literature if poems usually emerged fully formed in the poet's mind. First drafts are very rarely last drafts. Most artists are obsessive revisers, their original manuscripts often being mazes of corrections, notes and revisions. Those of James Joyce are famously labyrinthine. Indeed, if an artist were never to feel any sense of agency, we would think of them not so much as free but in the grip of an automatic compulsion. There is a difference between an artist who does not know where all her ideas come from and an autistic savant, for example, who simply pours out paintings or musical compositions without any self-consciousness. One such artist is the painter Seth Chwast. His art 'just comes out of him', says his mother. 'Seth is like a fire: he burns hot, he burns fast, he is voracious.'[7] We rightly celebrate these gifts, but not as paradigmatic expressions of the kind of human freedom we desire.

The freedom we crave does seem to require some degree of conscious control and deliberation. Perry's management of his own unconscious creativity provides clues as to what this entails. 'Most ideas come into the corner of your eye as you're working, as a kind of spin-off of your thought processes,' he says. 'So for me the best ideas always come towards the end of a batch of work because I'm in a process. It's churning around, I'm more relaxed.'

Perry talks of ideas 'emerging', embracing the idea that our conscious minds do not originate many of our thoughts. For Perry, it's about opening the doors for ideas to walk in, not fashioning them from scratch. 'Pirsig in *Zen and the Art of Motorcycle Maintenance* talks of ideas as being like furry creatures coming out of the undergrowth and one will approach you and all the others will be checking to see how it's treated. If you dismiss an idea, then you're probably putting off other ones coming from that direction. I'm very aware of embracing an idea even if it seems stupid, making a note of it, and suddenly you find that channel is open. Often a whole important idea of mine stems from some fairly trivial doodle in a sketchbook somewhere.'

We can learn something important about free will from this. To be free is not always to be in conscious control, but it does require a critical role for the conscious mind: deciding which ideas to jot down and which to dismiss, which to mull over and which to sit on, and where to go to provide the best environment for the little furry creatures to emerge. Although the conclusions we reach after thinking

91

about something usually just 'pop out', there is a difference between this and all thoughts simply emerging without any prior conscious consideration at all. We do not need to be aware of all our thinking to think freely, but we do need to be aware of some of it.

Although this seems to be right, it's difficult to pin down what exactly the role of the conscious mind is here and why it matters. For instance, after I wrote the first draft of that previous paragraph I stopped and asked myself, 'Is that true?' I then stared into the distance and allowed my mind to process it unconsciously. At times, I was aware of considerations for and against, but there was nothing like a linear, internal debate going on, of which I was in control. Given that when we speak, our awareness of what we are saying is usually simultaneous with us saying it, it would be remarkable if our internal conversations were any more consciously directed. Perfectly clear, coherent inner monologues only happen in films and novels, never in the real world.

So although it is hard to say what exactly is meant by conscious deliberation, I think we can at least say that it does seem to matter that we can interrupt the flow of our own ideas and decide to check, revise or reject them. The person who cannot do this is not free, but running out of control.

Perry describes this interplay between the conscious and the unconscious as a kind of 'call and response'. He sees this as more typical than being 'in the zone', free from conscious, executive control. 'A good state to find myself in as an artist is that one where I'm listening to the radio, and I'm drawing away and everything is quite free-flowing. Ninety-nine per cent of the time, that's a fantasy. It's a struggle. I have to constantly pull back and look at it and say, is this any good? I have to put it in the context of the work, where I'm exhibiting it, the art world, the market. I have to pull back and say am I just reinventing the wheel, doing some old load of rubbish, because in the end I want it to be a good work. So the idea that it

In the zone

is this spontaneous splurging that just kind of shoots out of me is tosh. It's a constant call and response checking, agonising over every decision I make.'

Although artists are generally comfortable with the idea that their ideas arise from their unconscious minds, they tend not to like it when neuroscientists explain this in terms of the brain. David Eagleman has found people get 'pissed off' whenever it is suggested that creativity might be about brain processes. 'I happened to be on a panel of several artists and choreographers discussing creativity, and they got really angry about the idea it had anything to do with some organ in their body rather than "them".' But this is silly: they should just accept that 'they' are their bodies and brains, and it is no affront to their dignity as artists that neuronal firing is the underlying process by which their ideas get born.

As we have seen, the idea that we could have done otherwise is often assumed to be central to the notion of free will. However, creative work often lacks this sense of alternate possibilities, and not only because much of it is mysterious to its creator. Like many writers of fiction, Bradbury talks as though his characters and stories compel him to go down certain roads. In his description of writing the story 'The Veldt', Bradbury says: 'George and his wife go down the hall. I follow them, typing madly, not knowing what will happen next.' Similarly, revisiting the characters of *Fahrenheit 451* for a stage show, Bradbury wanted to know what had happened to them. 'I asked,' he wrote. 'They answered.'

Certainly artists are often aware of the multiplicity of choices before them. If a painter looks at her palette, she will often see more than one colour, and infinite ways of mixing the ones that are there. But knowing that *it is possible* to do otherwise does not mean that *you are able* to do otherwise. What really seems to matter for the artist is not that she could have chosen other than what she did, but that she can choose other than what others would choose for her or for themselves. To put it another way, the freedom <u>desired is the freedom to do as you do, not to do other than you might have done</u>.

I doubt whether many artists even think about nature and nurture determining their choices, or whether what they create is the inevitable consequence of their life histories. If you are simply trying to free the creative energy within you, it does not seem to matter where it comes from. As for being ultimately responsible for the ideas they have, how can that question arise when they admit not even knowing where many of those ideas come from?

It is true that artists usually feel that they require an absence of constraint of sorts. But this is the <u>absence of *external* constraint</u>: being told what they can or cannot create, or conforming to people's expectations. In other respects, <u>artists are always working with constraints</u>: of the medium, of resources, of time. Indeed, working within such constraints is vital for development. An artist does not believe that she can create just anything. Rather, she chooses to work on specific projects in specific media. Great artists <u>are always acting against the constraints of their inherited traditions and practices,</u> but at the same time they have to understand and absorb them to move on from them. Creativity is about making something new, but not from nothing. Originality has nothing to do with being the ultimate cause, totally free from the effects of history, society and peers.

It is this sense of context that Perry believes is missing from the romantic myth of creativity as a pure, spontaneous outpouring, 'not just one context but the whole history of your life, where you live, the time you're in, the influences'. When you understand all the constraints that frame an artist's work, her freedom 'comes down to a freedom to make a fairly limited amount of choices within the context of your life as a creative person'. This kind of conditioning, far from providing a limit on freedom, is essential for any meaningful creation to take place. Proof that even the greatest artists are severely limited in their choices comes from the work itself. 'Out of all the infinite choices that an artist could make, it's curious that their work still looks like their work.'

Rather than labouring under the illusion that he has complete freedom to create outside of any biographical, social or historical constraints, Perry deliberately uses these to fuel his work. For him, a lot of 'creation is reaction, especially now in the art world where there's this dizzying possibility, with an incredibly pluralist and anything goes art world'. Indeed, one 'tactic to deal with that freedom of choice' is 'to go to a museum and see something I want to copy. It may be seen as a reactionary way of dealing with it but I don't think you can sit there and ponder and hope an idea will come.' And just as his work always picks up from the particular moment in the history of art he occupies, so it also picks up from the particular moment in his autobiography at which he finds himself. 'I tend to start where I left off, no matter how long ago it was.' Perry never tries to create *ex nihilo*. 'That idea of the blank page is terrifying.'

It is striking how Perry embraces the very thing that free will sceptics fret about: the extent to which our present choices are conditioned by the past. 'My decisions about what is good are locked into my emotional history. So therefore I can't necessarily change. I couldn't say, ooh, I'd love to think that was good. I can't do that because my emotional response to my next move is changing, but no way is it changing as fast as the actual things I'm doing. Therefore the likelihood is that I'm on a kind of rail that's related to all the other things that I've liked in the past. The thought that, yes, I could do anything but I wouldn't want to, is the thought that I feel. I'm locked into my preferences, style and history, and the things that I make will always relate – sometimes positively and sometimes negatively – to what I've done before. There'll be a call and response.'

Such constraints are the precondition for meaningful creation, not an obstacle to it. Perry quotes his wife, the psychotherapist Philippa Perry, who says, 'Sanity lies between rigidity and chaos.' For him, art is the same: 'I choose my path between rigidity and chaos.' And that too is surely a good definition of human freedom, the path between being robots without any self-regulation or autonomy and being butterflies for whom every choice arises randomly, unconditioned.

reflection

You do not achieve freedom by being the author of your own preferences and wants. You find freedom by being able to reflect on, endorse and express those preferences and wants. For instance, Perry is famously a transvestite, but that was not a desire he chose, or would have wanted to have chosen. 'Many transvestites or anyone with an unusual sexuality might feel it's a curse, because you're compelled to do something that might disrupt your marriage, that's expensive, that's embarrassing. For some people it might even be illegal.' His freedom to be a transvestite in no way implies a freedom to choose his preferences and desires from scratch. Perry agrees. 'Having that weird, abstract, ultimate freedom would be like being one of those people who's got no short-term memory, who is constantly "who am I and what do I want", and that's terrifying, a nightmare.'

In one sense, then, artistic freedom can be understood in terms of the metaphor of the rail that Grayson repeatedly uses. 'My own free will is running on rails,' he says. 'I'm under no illusion, I'm not suddenly going to start making boring twenty-eight-minute video art because my personality wouldn't allow it.'

To run along rails would appear to be the very antithesis of freedom, implying as it does the inability to follow any other course but the one you're on. But however paradoxical it sounds, there is a freedom in being able to run along your own rails, not to have to follow tracks which others push you onto.

This is illustrated in a remark in a monograph Perry makes about a work called 'Our Father': 'I bypassed any narrative and just went with my instinct.'[8] For the first time he felt he was simply doing what he did, undistracted by thoughts of what he ought to be doing, 'not to try to be dashingly original or on point', just 'to enjoy making a thing almost as a doodle, as a hobby, without the intent of it Getting A Message Across To The Audience', he told me. 'I indulged my makery enjoyment. I was bathing in my own sensual enjoyment of making things. That, in a way, though, is giving up even more to the tramlines.'

I think this shows that the kind of freedom that really matters is at root the freedom to allow your own talents, preferences and desires to flourish. As I've already suggested and will further discuss in the next chapter, for this to be freedom in the full sense, there must be some reflection on, control over and endorsement of the desires, beliefs and values you have. But there is no need whatsoever for us to be the originating author of any of these.

If that's true, then some of the most important factors in developing our freedom are practical rather than metaphysical. When I asked Perry what would make him feel as if he was losing his freedom, for example, he had to think for a while, before answering, 'I suppose an obvious one is just economic. If you run out of money to make things and a market to sell them to then I'd have to get a proper job. I have the freedom to make a living from my work, and I thank the art market daily for being such a good supplier of cash.' A little later he added, 'I suppose the biggest constriction on any human being is time. And health.'

For those used to metaphysical extravagance, time, money and health might seem rather mundane. But surely it is true that we cannot fully develop or express our freedom if we are wholly occupied earning a living, or are too ill even to think clearly. These are obvious truths that could only be missed by those so accustomed to comfort that they can take them for granted. Being well and comfortably off are not sufficient conditions for full human freedom, but they are necessary for achieving more than the minimum of it.

That's another reason why political and metaphysical freedom can only be separated artificially. The free will debate needs a social as well as a metaphysical context. 'If you had this discussion with an artist who was in Syria or Burma, or something like that, I'm sure it would be very different,' said Perry. And as the dissidents we are about to meet would verify, Perry is also right to say that freedom is like identity, in that it 'is only an issue when there's a problem with it'.

Although I have presented the absence of conscious control as in no way diminishing the creativity and authorship of the artist, some trends in twentieth-century thought might push us in the other direction. In various ways, the idea of the individual as an autonomous agent has been challenged in the twentieth century and into the twenty-first. Perhaps most famously, in 1967 Roland Barthes proclaimed 'the death of the author' in an essay of the same name. His idea was that the text or work of art had to be seen as existing in its own right. Once created, it had a life of its own, and the intentions of its creator were irrelevant.

Barthes's idea did not emerge from a vacuum. The diminished focus on the author in literary appreciation was linked to a wider tendency to proclaim the 'death of the self'. The Enlightenment ideal of the rational individual, sovereign of himself, was being gradually eroded by an increased awareness of the often irrational forces beyond our conscious control that shape our behaviour. Freud's writings at the beginning of the twentieth century did the most to spread this view, and it did not take long for his once-radical ideas to form the basis of the new common sense. Dale Carnegie's 1936 bestselling *How to Win Friends and Influence People*, for example, rested on the assumption that people's actions could be manipulated in ways of which they were not aware. Psychology would continue to catalogue the unconscious drivers of thought and action. For intellectuals of Barthes's generation, we did not appear to be captains of our own ships, but passengers in a vessel which was not of our making and whose direction was set by the winds and tides of fate.

Neuroscience has only fuelled this scepticism. As Michael Gazzaniga notes, 'no central command centre keeps all the other brain systems hopping to the instruction of a five-star general', which means, 'There is no one boss in the brain. You are certainly not the boss of the brain.'[9]

The idea that the self is an illusion is closely connected to the idea that free will is an illusion. The question of what the self is and whether it is an illusion is literally the subject of another book, one I wrote several years ago.[10] But the outlines of an answer can be given here and have indeed been suggested by the argument so far. It is a mistake to think of the self as some kind of unified 'pearl' at the core of our being. If we think the self is a kind of thing, such as an immaterial soul or a command and control centre in the brain, then we will be disappointed to find that it doesn't exist.

But this is not the only way to think about the self. The alternative is sometimes mockingly called the 'bundle' view, adopting a word David Hume used. The idea here is that the self is not a single thing that *has* thoughts, experiences, beliefs and sensations. Rather, it *is* an ordered collection of thoughts, experiences, beliefs and sensations.

This may sound less strange when we realise that everything else of any complexity in the universe is exactly the same. Water, for example, is not a thing that has two hydrogen atoms and one oxygen atom attached to it. Rather, it is something that comes into existence when hydrogen and oxygen fuse in the right way. Similarly, although we say colloquially that a watch *has* hands, a face, a glass and a mechanism, no one thinks that the watch is anything other than the sum of its parts. Everything that exists, apart from the most basic sub-atomic particles, is an ordered collection of parts. The self is no different. It is not to be found deep in the hidden recesses of the brain or lurking behind the body in some immaterial soul. It is rather something that emerges from the complex interaction of brain and body.

If you accept this view, as surely you must, then it should be evident that the self is not some single, unified executive consciousness that controls everything we do. The self has many parts, some conscious, some unconscious. What ties it together is that these parts create a kind of unity and harmony. Memory plays a key role, but so too does a reasonable degree of stability of personality, values, beliefs and intentions. In this way, the 'soul [is] greater than the hum of its parts' as Douglas Hofstadter memorably put it.[11]

The death of the self has been proclaimed prematurely. What is dead is the idea of the self as a simple, single, unified inner core of being. But understood properly, as the individual that emerges from a complex network of thoughts, sensations, beliefs and desires, it is very much alive. It is like an orchestra without a conductor, a jazz band, if you like, where each player is in sufficient harmony with the others to create a melodious, single tune. It should come as no surprise that this self often works in mysterious ways. It is not perfectly transparent to itself, and nor is it the author of its own being, whatever that might mean. But just as long as what we think, feel, believe and do forms some sort of coherent whole, which can in important ways direct itself, the self exists and is free to do what it wants.

Thinking about the freedom of the artist should change how we see the free will of everyone. First of all, artists help us to understand that to be free is for your choices to flow from you, whether they are entirely conscious or not. Second, to be free is to be able to generate highly personal outputs from the inputs of nature, nurture and society, not to be free from their influences, able to create from nothing. Free choices are ones where the individual contributes something indispensable to the choice, even if the ability to make that contribution is something that is in one sense simply the result of nature and all past experience – for what else could it be the result of? Third, to be free is to make choices in the knowledge that there are other options and without being forced or coerced one way or another. This can be the case even if, from a certain point of view, the choice you actually make is the only one you would ever have made in that situation.

This provides us with a different place to start thinking about what freedom means, and how it might be compatible with the unarguable facts at the heart of the case against it. We do not need to assert what neuroscience has made problematic: that a free choice must not be determined or even too conditioned by its past causes; that free choice has to be the result of a conscious decision; and in order for the idea to choose freely to exist, it must always have been possible that you could have done otherwise. Rather, what seems to be central is autonomy and lack of coercion, an ability to act free from the prescriptions of others and of convention. Free will, which has been made to appear so mysterious and elusive by philosophers and neuroscientists, is perfectly comprehensible and real if seen through the eyes of the creative artist.

5

The Dissident

The restaurant Ognisko, in the affluent borough of Kensington in London, has a special role in Europe's history of political liberty. It is part of the the Polish Hearth Club, founded in 1940 as a centre for Poles exiled from their home country after the Nazi invasion. It continued in this role throughout the Cold War, and remains a centre for the capital's Polish community. Although choosing what to eat from a menu is hardly the highest expression of human freedom, Ognisko was a fitting venue to discuss free will with a group of people who have all experienced a lack of political liberty. For anglophone philosophers who ponder freedom of the will, however, political freedom is an entirely distinct subject. Look at the entry for 'free, freedom' in the *Oxford Companion to Philosophy* and you will be directed to 'two groups of entries'. One includes political freedom, liberty, liberalism, self-determination, freedom of speech and imperialism. The other gathers together all the central ideas concerning what is sometimes called 'metaphysical freedom', such as freedom and determinism, scientific determinism, the will, compatibilism and incompatibilism, responsibility, fatalism and destiny.[1] In the anglophone tradition, political freedom concerns the structures of society that prevent us from, or enable us to, believe what we want, say what we want and do what we want. Free will (metaphysical freedom), on the other hand, is the capacity all humans may or may not have to make such choices freely in the first place. If, for example, you think that all our choices are determined by our genes, then you may conclude that no one has free will, whether they live in North Korea or South Dakota.

The orthodoxy is that political freedom and free will are two different things, and that one sheds no light on the other. But I'm not convinced this rigid separation is right. After all, as scholar of ancient philosophy Michael Frede points out, the Greek word for free will is *eleutheria*, the primary meaning of which is liberty. 'As the very term indicates,' says Frede, 'it must be a notion formed by analogy to the political notion of freedom.'[2] My Polish lunch was an attempt to dig a little deeper and discover what, if anything, the insights of those who have experienced deprivations of political liberty could contribute to our understanding of free will.

Around the table were Andrei Aliaksandrau, a journalist from Belarus, which as he says is 'known as the last true dictatorship in Europe'; the journalist Ismail Einashe, who came as a refugee to Britain when he was ten years old, the son of a Somali anti-government activist during the time of his country's dictatorship; Rahela Sidiqi, a women's and human rights activist who lived in Afghanistan under the Taliban; and Ma Jian, a Chinese novelist whose books have been banned in his home country.

Listening to their stories, it seemed to me that they all concerned ways in which the structures of society can make it impossible – or at least very difficult – to exercise some of the human capacities that make us free individuals. Among Sidiqi's 'principles of living' are 'to be honest, to provide services to humanity, to be kind to people, to help poverty'. These are capacities she believes we ought to develop because we are in this world to help humanity. Although she thinks this is a god-given duty, according to her faith, 'God never puts you

103

in chains if you don't do it. He leaves it to yourself, if you want to practise it or if you don't practise it. There are some things that you do, but God never blocks you.' Under the Taliban, however, it was not possible to develop these capacities freely. In particular, it was not possible to help that half of humanity with two X chromosomes to fulfil their potential. And so her political ideal is that 'human beings would be free in the way that God has created us'.

Aliaksandrau also talks of restrictions of freedom in terms of blocks. At the time of our conversation, Alexander Lukashenko had been president of Belarus for twenty years, trying 'to run the country as his own company, a family business, and all political rights are quite restricted'. Although not as brutal a regime as some dictatorships, people have been kidnapped, killed and held as political prisoners. 'As a journalist I experience restrictions and repressions because of what the government does and says. Keeping control over information or over the system of how information is circulated in society is the key to keeping power,' says Aliaksandrau. 'That is why journalists and social activists are blocked from fulfilling their duties, working freely and speaking freely.'

Aliaksandrau and Sidiqi's experiences illustrate the most straightforward link between political and metaphysical freedom: free will involves the capacity to do certain things by our own volition, and the right political structures need to be in place in order to express those capacities. Political freedom is thus the external condition of fully expressing an internal capacity we all have.

If you push this idea a little further, I think you can see how those internal capacities are not just there, whether we are able to express them or not. Political structures can actually affect how much free will we have, since what we are able to do is deeply tied up with our natures as social beings, embedded in particular cultures and times.

Take, for instance, the capacity to make political choices,

expressed most obviously at the ballot box. 'Back in 2010 when I was in Somaliland for the general election,' says Einashe, 'a lot of people were queuing up in the villages, going to vote. You could say they were exercising their freedom there, but the majority of them were illiterate, so were they making an informed choice? If you don't have equality and education, how can you possibly be informed? If people don't have the education and the economic means, how can they ultimately determine things for themselves?'

Similarly, Sidiqi believes that when women in rural Afghanistan choose to cover their faces they are not usually acting under a condition of freedom, because the alternative is not an option in their communities. A person who is more informed and educated has more capacity to make choices for herself, and therefore has a more developed free will.

This echoes the familiar distinction Isaiah Berlin made between positive and negative freedom: absence of constraint or coercion as opposed to having the means to pursue certain goods.[3] A person dumped in the middle of the desert has the negative freedom to walk out of it, because no one is standing in his way. But without shade, water and food to convert this into a positive freedom, this is meaningless.

The distinction between positive and negative freedom is usually taken to be a purely sociopolitical one. But it surely applies more broadly than this. A person who lacks education and information may have plenty of negative freedom, but they lack what is essential to make the most of that freedom in the positive sense. Their capacity for free will is in this respect underdeveloped. People's capacities to be free can be hampered in other ways too, some purely psychological. There is nothing in the external world preventing a person with agoraphobia from going where he likes, for example, but his fears mean that his free will is diminished in an important, though relatively minor way.

This introduces a vitally important consideration when thinking about free will which I'll come back to later: that it is a matter of degree. It is not something that we do or do not have. Just as societies cannot be divided neatly into the politically free and the not free, but lie on a spectrum between absolute tyranny and whatever the freest kind of society possible is, so human beings have varying degrees of freedom.

Unlike other animals, humans cannot only do what they want, they can ponder their own wants and question their own preferences. But we can't all do this to the same extent. If we have no access to education, and rely on information passed on to us by those with more power, we do not have as much of this freedom as we might. If we have not developed our powers of critical thinking, we may not be aware of all the options we have. And if we are ignorant of the various kinds of psychological biases and distortions of thought that humans are prone to, we are more likely to fall prey to them. Some of these limitations are the direct result of oppressive political structures. So there is a sense here in which an absence of political freedom can limit our freedom of thought, deliberation and choice. The political limits the personal; the public conditions the private.

Free will is not something either present or absent, but something we have in degrees. You build your freedom step by step, and you may overcome one barrier to freedom – political, social, economic, educational, psychological, historical – only to encounter another. As Aliaksandrau put it, 'It's not a state, it's a process.'

It does not of course follow that if the political structures of society allow you to exercise your capacities of free will, then you necessarily will. That's why the group at Ognisko gave a collective sigh and a nod when I asked whether they thought people in Britain took full advantage of their opportunities to exercise their freedom. 'When I sometimes look at the British press, at what

British politicians say, I realise that people don't value what they have,' says Aliaksandrau. 'They were born into democracy, they never had to fight for it, they take it for granted and they don't value anything that is given to them for free for which they don't pay personally.'

Jean-Paul Sartre made a similar point in typically hyperbolic fashion when he wrote that the French were 'never more free than during the German occupation'. This seems perverse, especially since he says that during that time, 'We had lost all our rights, beginning with the right to talk.' But it was only under those conditions that people truly realised how significant every small free act or thought was. 'Because the Nazi venom seeped even into our thoughts, every accurate thought was a conquest. Because an all-powerful police tried to force us to hold our tongues, every word took on the value of a declaration of principles. Because we were hunted down, every one of our gestures had the weight of a solemn commitment.' Instead of acting without thinking and taking freedom for granted, people came to realise how much of what they did presented an opportunity either to knowingly exercise freedom or to go with the flow and deny one's own freedom. 'And the choice that each of us made of his life and of his being was an authentic choice because it was made face to face with death, because it could always have been expressed in these terms: "Rather death than . . ."'[4]

For those in our lunch party, this was putting it too strongly. 'I don't believe you become freer when you're oppressed,' said Ma Jian. 'Look at North Korea. When you say I don't have the freedom to go back to China, you cannot invert that and say I have the freedom not to go to China.'

Aliaksandrau also takes issue with Sartre. 'You don't become freer when you are oppressed, but you start really appreciating freedoms when they're under threat or when you actually lose them. The declaration of human rights was adopted after the Second

World War when the whole of humanity saw what it is like when you don't have freedom and you don't have rights. People were terrified of what happened. Unfortunately, human beings need tragedy to start thinking.'

I agree that Sartre is excessive in his claim. But he is onto something, namely that to be truly free as a human being requires more than the absence of constraint. You have to use your own capacity to make choices, and accept responsibility for your own decisions. In that sense, it is indeed possible to become more acutely aware that you do have fundamental choices to make when restrictions are placed on them, and you can let your free will muscles atrophy when things become easy.

But there is nothing about living under oppression that automatically makes one more aware of one's freedom. People can go with the flow of oppression as much as they do with freedom. It's a bit like being a bird that has become cage-bound, so used to confinement that it fears the mere possibility of flying freely beyond it. Even being a dissident can become a habit that takes the power resisted as a permanent given. 'You know about all the restrictions and limitations, and you know for sure you can go to prison for some things you say or do, be forced to leave the country or lose your job,' says Aliaksandrau. 'But I can see people who choose this path despite this threat. And I think it's interesting, it's kind of dangerous maybe, that we start taking this danger for granted. It's like the rules of the game. It's so naturally a part of your life that you can just go on with it.'

We do not always recognise the scope of our own freedom, at least in part as a consequence of the social structures around us. Sidiqi recalls some of her community development work in Afghanistan, which required the women involved to use a walkie-talkie. After a while, one told Sidiqi she didn't want to use it any more because 'my people all say that I'm "kafir" now'. Sidiqi's role then was to try to make the woman see that she did in fact have a choice. 'You know that you're doing good work, helpful for your people,' she told her. 'It's not a problem if they say something. They are not hitting you.'

That illustrates one of the most sinister aspects of totalitarian societies: their capacity to mould our thinking in ways we are not even aware of. 'It's like a shadow, like brainwashing, you don't even see it,' says Ma Jian. He sees this at work with writers who have remained in China and who have in sometimes subtle ways altered their writing as a result. 'If you are a writer, you choose to write,' he says, and to do so requires him to remain in exile, 'because I've seen how other writers in China are writing with restrictions, and I would become like them if I went back. That would be terrible. When you are further away from the mountain, you see it more clearly.'

Our capacity to exercise our free will can be limited by circumstances in sometimes surprising ways. Einashe, for instance, argues that 'in Somalia women have more rights to choose what they wear than they do in Britain' because the Somali community in the UK is much more conservative. Nonetheless, as Sidiqi's example shows, often there is a choice that can be made, and that is really a choice to use and develop our freedom or not. *develop freedom*

The discussion at Ognisko made it clear to me that the capacity to exercise and develop our free will is not entirely under our own control, or simply a matter of attitude. To fully develop our free will requires political freedom and favourable social structures. The freest person both wholly utilises his or her own capacities of choice and deliberation, and is not excessively constrained by society. When either of these conditions is absent, our freedom is diminished; if neither is fulfilled, we have none at all.

There is another aspect of received opinion about free will that our discussion over lunch challenged. Paradigmatic examples of free will in the philosophical literature often centre around simple choices. You opt for *barszcz*, the famous beetroot soup, but you could have picked *trzaski*, crispy pork crackling. The emphasis is on the ability to do other than what you actually do. As we have already seen, 'could have done otherwise' is often taken by both philosophy and common sense as the core definition of a free choice.

And yet when people stand up for political freedom, it more often looks like a case of could *not* have done otherwise. Take Paul Rusesabagina, who protected 1,268 Hutu and Tutsi refugees during the Rwandan Genocide in the hotel he managed. It seems he could have fled and saved his own skin instead. But he did not. After a while, however, he did decide to send his wife and children to safety. 'Tatiana and the children were angry that I wasn't going with them,' he later said. 'I told them I was the only person who could negotiate for the people in the hotel. If I left, they would be killed, and I would never be a free man. I'd be a prisoner of myself, never able to eat and feel satisfied or go to bed and rest. I'd be a traitor.'[5]

Although it appears Rusesabagina had a choice, that is not how it seemed to him. He felt very strongly that in the position he was in, he really had no choice. If he walked away, he would not be able to live with himself.

It is common for people who sacrifice their own well-being or safety for human rights and social causes to feel like this. After all, if we really could choose to change our convictions and values by mere acts of will, why would any dissident not do so and avoid persecution? Sidiqi, for example, stands up for women's rights. But she does not feel that rejecting them is an option, and she agrees with my suggestion that there is a sense in which she feels she must stick by them.

Similarly, Aliaksandrau says, 'For me, when we talk about political freedoms, it's not even a choice, it's the only natural thing. I can't think, "Shall I go to thinking that freedom of expression is very bad?" No! It's not even an option.' The most meaningful choices are often the ones that we feel we must make, in order to retain our integrity. Free choices can thus be in one way compelled. This does not make them in any way less admirable. '"I cannot tell a lie" and "He couldn't hurt a fly" are not exemptions from praiseworthiness but testimonies to it,' as the philosopher Susan Wolf puts it. 'If one feels one "has no choice" but to speak out against injustice, one ought not to be upset about the depth of one's commitment.'[6]

Although it might seem odd to think of people being free when they are in some sense compelled to act a certain way, Wolf neatly turns this doubt around when writing about the extent to which our interests determine what we do. 'Consider first what it would mean for the agent's actions not to be determined by his interests,' she asks. 'This would mean, I think, that the agent has the ability to act against everything he believes in and everything he cares about.' The oddity of this is not hard to draw out. 'Though perhaps he loves his wife, it must be possible for him not to love her. Though perhaps he cares about people in general, it must be possible for him not to care. This agent, moreover, could not have reasons for his interests – at least no reasons of the sort we normally have. He cannot love his wife, for example, because of the way his wife is – for the way his wife is is not up to him.'[7]

In this view, it is actually essential that good actions are in some sense determined in order for us to make sense of them. What matters is simply that they are 'rightly determined' by the 'right sorts of interests' for the 'right sorts of reasons'. But if they are not determined by anything, they cannot be good or right. They become events that just happen.

The idea that good people in some way have to do what they do has a long pedigree. According to Michael Frede, for Aristotle 'a wise and virtuous person cannot but make the choices he makes'.[8]

Nor does there seem to be any reason to think that praise is any less merited because he could not have done otherwise. 'If somebody does something remarkable, surely the merit lies in the accomplishment, not in the fact that the person could have chosen to do something quite unremarkable instead,' says Frede.[9]

The kind of choice where we really could equally go either way seems to be the least valuable kind of freedom. This can be illustrated by Buridan's Ass, a thought experiment named after the fourteenth-century French philosopher whose theories inspired it. Buridan believed that we will always choose whichever course of action we judge to be better. What then if 'two courses be judged equal'? In such cases, 'the will cannot break the deadlock, all it can do is to suspend judgement until the circumstances change, and the right course of action is clear'.[10]

Later thinkers identified a problem with this theory. If it were right, then what would a rational hungry and thirsty ass do when placed equidistant between a bucket of water and a stack of hay? Since it has no reason to go to the water or hay first, and since it is perfectly rational, it would 'suspend judgement', stay where it is and starve. Of course, in this situation we would not starve. We would exercise our free will to go to one and then the other.

This liberty of indifference, the freedom to make a random choice when there are no good reasons to prefer one or the other, is of course very valuable. But many think that it is the very lowest grade of freedom. Descartes, for example, writes that 'indifference does not belong to the essence of human freedom, since not only are we free when ignorance of what is right makes us indifferent, but we are also free – indeed at our freest – when a clear perception impels us to pursue some object'.[11] Freedom to flip a coin is not as important as the freedom to understand the pros and cons and feel moved to act accordingly.

For freedom to be meaningful it must not be the ability just to

Identity

choose anything. To be free is to be able to express one's fundamental values, to live according to the identity one has. And yet these values and these identities are not things we choose in any straightforward way. 'If I'm honest,' says Einashe, 'most of my life has been spent living a life defined by a culture and by a faith that I didn't choose.' Of course these things do not set our identities and values in stone. 'Much of my own personal struggle has been choosing myself to say that I could be secular, I could be humanist, I could be liberal,' he says. But such struggles do not start from a clean slate. We make our choices from within situations that we did not choose, asserting values we acquired and which we often feel force themselves upon us. 'We cannot separate free will from the wider context of the influence of others and the environment,' as Sidiqi put it.

Aliaksandrau summed it up well. 'Pure free will does not exist because of all the influences we get throughout life, even because we're born in this particular country, in this particular century, with these particular parents. There are things that we're not really choosing.'

Indeed, it is because being able to express one's unchosen identity is such an important freedom that the inability to live or work in your country of origin can be so painful. 'In exile, free will cannot exist,' says Ma Jian. 'Free will is impossible when one is denied the freedom to return to one's homeland.' When your passport is taken, something of you is taken too. You are not complete, and cannot express yourself fully. 'Being a national of a country or being part of a nation is such a part of your identity that living in exile restricts your identity in some way,' as Aliaksandrau puts it.

That is why communities in exile can in some ways be more distinctly of their nation than ones back in the homeland. Aliaksandrau offers as an example the small Belarusian community set up in London after the Second World War by people who had never actually lived in the Soviet Union. 'What I found very interesting was that when I moved to London two years ago and joined this Belarusian community, I felt there is more Belarus in this than in my country because of the restrictions.' They speak more Belarusian and celebrate more national holidays than they do in Belarus. 'So I kind of fulfilled my identity more being in exile in comparison to what I could do in my country.'

Identity provides another example of how free choices can be compelled, and so there is no simple opposition between freedom and necessity. Consider how Aliaksandrau talks about his free choice to speak Belarusian. 'Being a Belarusian is a very important part of my identity, and for me to be free includes to be free to speak my native language,' he says. 'But it's a choice. I wasn't born into the environment where speaking the native language is a natural process, unfortunately.' However, he also says that 'it became my choice because my personal identity required it of me'. There is a necessity here, but it is not the oppressive necessity of yielding to the will of another.

Freedom of belief is therefore freedom to think for oneself. This has nothing to do with our beliefs being independent of the causal history of our lives or our cultures. Indeed, it assumes the opposite: beliefs that cannot be explained at least in part by the life experiences that inform them are not beliefs worth having. This strengthens my conviction that political and metaphysical freedoms are parts of the same whole, not distinct capacities.

This line of thinking illuminates the role of conscious thought in freedom. Conscious deliberation is indeed important for the formation of our beliefs. We do not think that people who believe what they do without any reflection on it are paradigms of human freedom. That's why education and information are so important for developing freedom: if we are not able to assess and revise the values and beliefs we inherit, we are not truly free. But it is also the case that a lot of the processing of ideas goes on unconsciously, and that when we decide one way or another, the decision often seems to pop into our heads, rather than arrive as the inevitable 'therefore' at the end of a chain of reasoning. People like Rusesabagina and Sidiqi do not experience their strong commitments as conclusions of arguments but as core elements of their being. Conscious thought therefore has a role in human freedom, but it is a much more complicated one than simply the idea that only conscious thought alone can produce free choices and freely held beliefs.

Brains and genes have been largely absent from our discussion of artists and dissidents as paradigms of free will. Once you focus on what meaningful free will comprises, such things become irrelevant. When we understand how artistic and political freedoms work, we see clearly that there is no need to think of choices as undetermined by prior events or independent of brain activity. Nor do we have to think of free agents as ultimately responsible for being the people they are. When we think about how artists and dissidents operate, none of the histrionic cries from those who deny free will have any force. The fact that the brain in some sense produces ideas, beliefs, desires and actions is besides the point, because no one is claiming that they come from some free-floating self. In the case of both the artist and the dissident, it is apparent how much of who we are and what we do is given. Freedom cannot be the ability to build a life and to make choices from scratch.

To be free is for one's decisions, actions, beliefs and values to be one's own. We are more free to the extent that we are more self-directed, running along our own tracks rather than on those laid down by others. For this to be the case there needs to be a significant contribution from conscious thought at some stage in the process. But that does not mean every action, every thought, must be the product of a deliberation. All of this should be clear in general terms, and more of the detail will be worked out shortly when we see how freedom is diminished.

We have also seen that since freedom is not absolute, it is a matter of degree. Our mistake is often to think of 'the will' as a capacity that we exercise or not, and is therefore absent or present. It is better to think of freedom as something we have more or less of. And this explains why there is never a knock-down discovery that proves we do not have free will. Going back to the science, we discover that in every case where free will is denied, what is shown is merely that we have *less* control in many circumstances than we think we do. And it is precisely because such judgements are always comparative that we can understand the difference between patho-logical and normal cases: again something we will be looking at in more detail shortly.

Not only is freedom a matter of degree, it has several different components. Freedom can involve more or less spontaneity, origi-nality, conscious deliberation and independence from the control of others. These elements can be present in different degrees. What an artist lacks in conscious control she can make up for in originality; what the dissident might lack in originality she can make up for in independence from the control of others. Freedom is not one thing: it is a cluster of capacities. But these capacities are things we really have, and nothing we have learnt from science can take them from us.

PART FOUR

Freedom Diminished

6

The Psychopath

The philosopher Daniel Dennett describes free will as 'the most difficult and the most important philosophical problem confronting us today'.[1] When I asked him why, he told me: 'It's important because of the long-standing tradition that free will is a prerequisite for moral responsibility. So our system of law and order, of punishment and praise and blame, promise-keeping, promise-making, law of contracts, criminal law – all of this depends on one notion or another of free will.' However, we now have 'neuroscientists, physicists and philosophers saying that science has shown us that free will is an illusion and then not shrinking from the implication that our systems of law are built on foundations of sand and this cannot hold: we're going to have to have a radical reformation and the world is going to be hugely changed.'

The root of the problem is the now familiar 'could have done otherwise' condition for free will. As we have seen, we may be able to understand an action as free in some sense even if we could not have done otherwise. But can we consider a person blame- or praiseworthy if they could not have done otherwise? To many, the answer seems obviously to be no. As neuroscientist Sam Harris says of rapists and murderers, 'To say that they were free not to rape and murder is to say that they could have resisted the impulse to do so (or could have avoided feeling such an impulse altogether) – with the universe, including their brains, in precisely the same state it was in at the moment they committed their crimes.'[2] Harris takes as an example Joshua Komisarjevsky, who with his accomplice broke into a family home, beat the father, raped and sexually assaulted the mother and daughters, doused his victims in gasoline and set them alight. Harris says, 'If I had truly been in Komisarjevsky's shoes on July 23, 2007 – that is, if I had his genes and life experience and an identical brain (or soul) in an identical state – I would have acted exactly as he did.' The fact that he did not have his genes and life experience was no more than an accident of birth and circumstance. 'The role of luck, therefore, appears decisive.'[3] Therefore, 'Anyone born with the soul of a psychopath has been profoundly unlucky.'[4]

Richard Dawkins is another scientist who has argued that 'a truly scientific, mechanistic view of the nervous system makes nonsense of the very idea of responsibility, whether diminished or not. Any crime, however heinous, is in principle to be blamed on antecedent conditions acting through the accused's physiology, heredity and environment … Assigning blame and responsibility is an aspect of the useful fiction of intentional agents that we construct in our brains as a means of short-cutting a truer analysis of what is going on in the world in which we have to live.' Dawkins argues that our current way of thinking makes as little sense as Basil Fawlty thrashing his broken-down car as punishment in a classic episode of *Fawlty Towers*. 'Don't judicial hearings to decide questions of blame or diminished responsibility make as little sense for a faulty man as for a Fawlty car?' he asks. 'My dangerous idea is that we shall eventually grow out of all this and even learn to laugh at it, just as we laugh at Basil Fawlty when he beats his car. But I fear it is unlikely that I shall ever reach that level of enlightenment.'[5]

I think that if we ever started treating people in the same way as we did broken cars, it would not show that we had become enlightened but had in fact descended into a terrible darkness. It's true that we need to show more understanding of how criminal minds work, but if we do, we will find that though they force us to rethink the idea of responsibility, they do not destroy it.

One of the most notorious concentrations of psychopaths in the United Kingdom is Broadmoor in Berkshire. The moral and philosophical complexities of this institution, which opened as Broadmoor Criminal Lunatic Asylum in 1863, become evident as soon as you see it. With its windowless twenty-foot walls and watchtowers, the architecture screams 'prison'. But the signage says 'hospital'. It has patients, not inmates, and although many inside have committed terrible crimes, it is run not by Her Majesty's Prison Service but by West London Mental Health Trust. Don't ask if the occupants are mad or bad: they are both.

I had come to Broadmoor to talk to Dr Gwen Adshead, who as a consultant forensic psychotherapist is one of the institution's most senior psychiatrists. I started by asking the most basic question of all: why was Broadmoor a hospital rather than a prison? One of the main historical reasons, she replied, is the 'beneficent tradition that people who are mentally ill should not be imprisoned. It's about the people who are thought to be mentally ill at the time of their offending who deserve some sympathy – there's a sense of desert there.'

On reflection, I find this an extremely telling remark. It is often assumed that once you decide that a person's actions are not the result of the exercise of their free will, then it no longer makes sense to blame them for what they do. Desert goes out of the window, only to jump back in through another: if a person's actions were not the result of the exercise of their free will, then they do seem to deserve sympathy.

This doesn't only apply to the criminally insane. Edward Rees QC has defended many minors who have committed violent crimes, including murders. In a café near the Old Bailey in London, he told me about one who was just sixteen, a 'child' who got sentenced to twenty years, a 'terribly damaged kid' who 'never had a life' and 'was fucked from the moment he was born'. He wasn't mentally ill and didn't even have a conduct disorder. 'And there are lots of them like that. They're always from dysfunctional families. They're little buggers. But they've been made into what they are, they've been brutalised.' Like almost everyone who has worked with disadvantaged children who have ended up in prison, Rees can't help but see them as deserving sympathy. That does not mean refusing to hold such people to account. 'To abdicate all responsibility is a nonsense,' he says.

The reason, I think, why it is so hard to banish ideas of desert altogether is that to be human is to respond both emotionally and morally to each other, to have what philosopher P. F. Strawson describes as 'the non-detached attitudes and reactions of people directly involved in transactions with each other'.[6] Strawson argues that not only is it desirable that we have such responses, it would be futile to try to rid ourselves of them.

Our attitudes towards blame and sympathy are examples of this. Those who find themselves convinced that criminals could not have done otherwise do not give up all notions of desert, which is an example of the kind of 'reactive attitude' Strawson describes. Rather, they simply modify their sense of what this desert comprises, shifting from blame to sympathy. What no one does is give up the idea of desert altogether. To do so would require us to become morally and emotionally indifferent to others. This is not what people who believe it is wrong to blame anyone for wrongdoing really want. On the contrary, what they tend to advocate is a strong but different reactive attitude, one of deep compassion and sympathy.

Desert would therefore appear to be asymmetric: people can be thought to deserve sympathy but not blame. The asymmetry rests on the thought that you deserve blame for what is your fault and sympathy for what is not, and since nothing is ultimately anyone's fault, we can only deserve sympathy.

It does not follow from this that we abolish punishment. People may need to be locked up, for the protection of others or for their own rehabilitation. As the American philosopher Tamler Sommers puts it, 'Rapists and thieves are bad people. It may not be their fault that they are bad people, but they are bad people nonetheless.'[7] And bad people should be treated differently to good ones. But we can do this without blaming them for being bad. Indeed, knowing we have to do something unpleasant to them even though they are not to blame can deepen our sense of sympathy.

We can therefore have a sense of desert that does without ideas of ultimate responsibility and therefore also of blame. You deserve what is appropriate. It is 'suitable reward or punishment', and so is only loosely connected with responsibility. Someone deserves to be paid the appropriate wage for a job, for example, whether free will is an illusion or not.

Although this makes sense, I'm not yet convinced that we ought to get rid of the idea of blame altogether. If the notion of blame ever required 'ultimate responsibility', it was always incoherent, since we are the product of factors that are in part outside of our control and even predate our birth. But if we allow for an idea of partial responsibility, can it also make sense to attribute at least partial blame, and would it be good to do so? To answer this, we first have to consider the extent to which it makes sense to hold people responsible for their bad acts.

The discussion with political dissidents has shown us why free will is a matter of degree. This also becomes evident when you think about

child development. Conscious self-control requires a fully functioning prefrontal cortex, but as the neuroscientist Dick Swaab points out,
its development is 'a slow process, continuing at least until the age of
twenty-five. It's only at that age that an individual is fully equipped
to control their impulses and make moral judgements.'[8]

This implies that responsibility is also not all or nothing, something that becomes apparent when considering criminality. As
Broadmoor's Gwen Adshead puts it, 'There are people that we want
to condemn, and for them we need one sort of legal measure; and
there are people who we want to condemn a bit less. We don't want
to say they're completely lacking any agency, such as they can't be
condemned, but we can also see that if we were in their situation,
having had all their disadvantages, that we might also not want to
blame them quite so much. I think the diminished responsibility
defence fits neatly into that.'

That legal phrase, 'diminished responsibility', captures a truth
about free will far better than most metaphysical jargon. The people
in Broadmoor are not completely lacking the capacities necessary for
free will. It's just that they do not have them all, or they are not fully
functioning. Agency, and so responsibility, is diminished, not absent.
There is no binary distinction between those who have diminished
or full responsibility. Rather, it is as Adshead puts it, 'a sliding scale',
one on which individuals can move. One woman Adshead worked
with, for example, was obviously in a very disturbed state of mind
when she hurt her month-old baby, but she was cool and collected
enough when Adshead saw her earlier on the day we met.

The ways in which aspects of responsibility can be present even
in extreme psychotic cases is evident in the case of another woman
Adshead worked with who killed a social worker whom she believed
to be the devil. At her trial she got an insanity verdict, quite rightly
in Adshead's view. However, 'She did know that she was killing, and
she did know that killing was wrong, and she did spend three hours

in a room deciding whether to do it or not.' What's more, she felt guilty about it, and 'found it very difficult that the clinical team were telling her it was not her fault because she was psychotic at the time'.

Indeed, although the general public's perception of patients at Broadmoor is of people who are beyond all notions of responsibility and blame, for Adshead working with them requires such notions to be at the heart of discussions. As she put it in one of her papers, 'I want to both respect [the patient's] autonomy as an individual and help her regain autonomy in terms of acting more safely in the future. I have to treat her as a person with intentions and actions.'[9]

However, although the law does seem to get it right when it talks of diminished responsibility, it conspires to maintain the pretence that the criminally insane are in a category of their own. Technically speaking, to accept a plea of insanity, rather than diminished responsibility, a jury needs to apply what is known as the M'Naghten test, named after the defendant in an 1843 trial which set the precedent. The House of Lords codified this in a ruling which stated 'that to establish a defence on the ground of insanity, it must be clearly proved that, at the time of the committing of the act, the party accused was labouring under such a defect of reason, from disease of the mind, as not to know the nature and quality of the act he was doing; or, if he did know it, that he did not know he was doing what was wrong'.[10]

'The M'Naghten test is rarely used,' says Adshead, 'because hardly anybody meets M'Naghten.' In practice, courts follow psychiatric reports, which try to determine whether a person was of sound mind. And in reality, this is always a matter of degree. The criminally insane are therefore not really in a category of their own, but just at the more extreme end of the spectrum of diminished responsibility.

Interestingly, Adshead reports that the nursing staff at Broadmoor are constantly distinguishing between patients whom they believe are sufficiently responsible to blame and those who just can't help themselves. 'So person A thumps them and they will be furious and say he's just a bad person who wanted to do that to make me feel bad. And person B will thump them and they'll say poor Jim, he's very mentally ill, he really didn't intend it. And they're doing these assessments all day, every day, so those intuitions are very strong.'

Adshead suggests that these distinctions are often based on whether people believe the perpetrator intended harm. 'I wonder whether we punish people for their intentions,' she says, 'whether they chose their intentions or not.' This identifies another factor – intention – which is involved in praise and blame but does not hinge on whether the intended action is ultimately freely chosen or not. The importance of intention is illustrated by a nice childhood story many of us will find familiar, that the QC Edward Rees told me. 'If I cocked up something and got blamed for it by my mother, I would say "But I didn't think", and she would often respond with, "That's just it: you don't think". And I always thought, well, if I didn't think about the consequence and therefore I didn't intend the consequence, how can I be blamed?' It is the absence of any intention to do wrong that makes us feel unjustly accused, not any sense that we could not have done otherwise.

Even Sam Harris, one of the most emphatic deniers of free will and with it notions of blame, recognises that, 'What we condemn most in another person is the conscious intention to do harm.' This makes sense, 'Because what we do subsequent to conscious planning tends to most fully reflect the global properties of our minds – our beliefs, desires, goals, prejudices, etc.'[11]

What is interesting about this notion of intention is that it genuinely does seem to be metaphysically neutral – that is to say, it makes sense to treat people as having intentions whether or not those intentions are inevitable, the product of chance or ultimately chosen.

Indeed, it may make sense even if people don't actually have intentions at all. This is at the heart of Daniel Dennett's idea of the 'intentional stance'. The intentional stance is not a belief about how other people, animals or even some machines, actually are. It is rather a strategy for dealing with them.

'Here is how it works,' writes Dennett in his book on the subject. 'First you decide to treat the object whose behaviour is to be predicted as a rational agent; then you figure out what beliefs that agent ought to have, given its place in the world and its purpose. Then you figure out what desires it ought to have, on the same considerations, and finally you predict that this rational agent will act to further its goals in the light of its beliefs.'[12]

Dennett's point is that this strategy works. More importantly, perhaps, it is the strategy people use when they are dealing with what they believe to be conscious creatures in control of their own behaviour. To treat someone as a conscious agent is just to adopt the intentional stance towards them. In material science, in contrast, we adopt the physical stance, treating atoms and particles as though their behaviour is predicted entirely by the laws of physics, which they are. When looking at plants, animals and technology we adopt the design stance, predicting how they will work on the basis of either how they are designed or how they have evolved – how nature has designed them, as it were.

There are times when we adopt the physical stance towards humans, such as when we want to calculate how long it will take a falling one to hit the ground if dropped from an aeroplane. A little more often we adopt the design stance, such as when we want to think about the effect of diet, exercise or environment on the health of the body. But when it comes to behaviour, we are almost always much more successful when we adopt the intentional stance.

The simplest explanation for why the intentional stance works is that people do indeed think, decide and intend. I think this must at some important level be true. But the beauty of the theory is that it applies even if people only act *as though* they think, decide and intend. Even if you buy into the most hard-line scientistic denial of free will and believe that all our actions are just the result of neurons firing, it is undeniable that you can interact with, affect and predict the behaviour of people much more successfully if you assume they think about what they do.

So even though both Adshead and Harris's comments imply that intentions are real, it would not matter in practice if there weren't a deep difference between people whose actions reflect their intentions and those who don't. The only difference that matters is whether people's actions seem to be intentional.

Intentions, in the form of good or ill will, provide the very foundations for P. F. Strawson's 'personal reactive attitudes', our moral and emotional responses to the behaviour of others. These 'rest on, and reflect, an expectation of, and demand for, the manifestation of a certain degree of goodwill or regard on the part of other human beings towards ourselves; or at least on the expectation of, and demand for, an absence of the manifestation of active ill will or indifferent disregard'.[13]

These attitudes also ground punishment. As Adshead says, we 'punish people for their intentions, whether they chose their intentions or not', because, as Harris says, 'To say I was responsible for my behaviour is simply to say that what I did was sufficiently in keeping with my thoughts, intentions, beliefs, and desires to be considered an extension of them.'[14] This way of thinking has an antecedent in Aristotle, as Michael Frede explains. According to Aristotle, 'for us to be responsible for what we do, our action has to somehow reflect our motivation', but that does not require us to postulate that our motivation is the product of free choice. 'Responsibility does not involve a will,' says Frede.[15]

This idea might sound fishy. The problem is that our intentions are said to matter whether we freely choose to have them or not, which is just as well since intentions are not, on the whole at least, freely chosen. But how can we be held responsible for our intentions if they are not themselves intentionally chosen? To put it another way, if we can only be held to account for what we do intentionally, but we do not intentionally choose our intentions, how can we be held to account for our intentions?

This is another of those questions that only appears to be problematic if we assume that the only real responsibility is ultimate responsibility. But holding people to account and even punishing them for what they intentionally do requires no belief in ultimate responsibility. All it requires is a recognition that they act badly because of something about the way they are – their harmful desires, beliefs or goals – rather than because of some mistake or some freak occurrence. Those who cause harm intentionally have ill wills and will do the same or similar again unless they change, unlike people who cause harm unintentionally and so only need to be shown the mistakes they have made so that they don't repeat them.

Although this does not justify pure retributive punishment, even 'hard incompatibilists' who reject all ideas of blame and responsibility acknowledge that it justifies the right kind of corrective punishment to deter, reform or protect. 'Instead of treating people as if they deserve blame,' argues Derk Pereboom, 'the hard incompatibilist can turn to moral admonition and encouragement, which presuppose only that the offender has done wrong.'[16]

If you still doubt that holding people responsible makes sense in such situations, Hume provides a compelling argument that it does. He completely inverts the sceptical challenge, arguing that the justification of punishment actually rests upon the person being punished having a character and intentions that they cannot simply alter at will. 'Hatred or anger,' he argues, are incited only when we observe a connection between 'criminal or injurious actions' and the person who commits them. If, however, we are at complete liberty to do whatever we choose, 'this connexion is reduced to nothing, nor are men more accountable for those actions'. That is because

> actions are by their very nature temporary and perishing; and where they proceed not from some cause in the character and disposition of the person, who performed them, they infix not themselves upon him, and can neither redound to his honour, if good, nor infamy, if evil. The action itself may be blameable; it may be contrary to all the rules of morality and religion: But the person is not responsible for it; and as it proceeded from nothing in him, that is durable or constant, and leaves nothing of that nature behind it, it is impossible he can, upon its account, become the object of punishment or vengeance. According to the hypothesis of liberty, therefore, a man is as pure and untainted, after having committed the most horrid crimes, as at the first moment of his birth, nor is his character any way concerned in his actions; since they are not derived from it, and the wickedness of the one can never be used as a proof of the depravity of the other.

Hence 'It is only upon the principles of necessity, that a person acquires any merit or demerit from his actions, however the common opinion may incline to the contrary.'[17]

Alexander of Aphrodisias had similar thoughts millennia before. He was considering the question of whether praise and blame should be directed at people who could equally well have chosen to do good or bad, or whether it should be directed at those whose goodness or badness made it inevitable that they behaved the way they did. He thought the first option led to a contradiction: the good could not be called good because they did not deserve praise for their good actions, and the bad could not be called bad because they don't merit blame. As he put the paradox, 'Being prudent and virtuous will not be in the power of those who are prudent and virtuous; for [such men] are no longer capable of receiving the vices opposite to their virtues. And the same point applies to the vices of bad men; for it is no longer in the power of such men to cease being bad.'[18]

The fact that people act on the basis of intentions, or merely that they act as though on the basis of intentions, is therefore a very good reason why we should indeed hold them responsible for what they do and even punish them. This is true even if intentions are not chosen or that, in some sense, people could not have done other than as they did.

Despite the claim that a lot rides on the philosophical debate about free will, abstract metaphysics is largely irrelevant when it comes to how we actually think about praise and blame, reward and punishment in daily life. People are not sent to Broadmoor because we believe they had the ultimate power to have been different. Rather, as Adshead puts it, 'the reason that people come here now is a kind of practical solution to a problem'. That problem is that 'the people who come here are the people who need this level of security. They're not coming here because they're especially wicked, they're coming here because they're not manageable anywhere else.'

This might point to more than how a particular aspect of the criminal justice system works. Perhaps there is a sense in which all of morality can be understood as being far more about the pragmatics of managing harm than we conventionally expect. This thought impressed itself upon me when I read Patricia Churchland's *Braintrust*, about the neural basis of moral thinking. Although this was a book about morality and moral thinking, going through the index I could find no entries for 'free will', 'responsibility', 'blame', 'autonomy' or 'choice'.

When I met Churchland and pointed this out to her, she said that she 'probably should have said more about it', and that the reason she didn't was simply that her central issue in the book was 'how it is that any organism will sacrifice its own interests for another and what that biologically looks like'. Nonetheless, the fact that it's possible to say so much about morality without mentioning these things, and without me noticing their absence the first time I read it, suggests that free will, blame and responsibility may not be as central to moral thinking as is usually supposed.

But how could that be so? For an answer, I went back to a previous interview I had conducted with Churchland about *Braintrust*. In that book, Churchland argued that 'what we humans call ethics or morality' is a 'scheme for social behaviour'.[19] So typically, 'For many of the social problems that people have to address, problems of scarcity of resources or what have you, they have to come together and negotiate and figure out an amicable solution so that they can carry on. Sometimes those solutions work out fairly well in the short run and then they have to modify them so they can work out in the longer run.'[20]

Because morality is essentially social problem-solving, different societies with different social problems have importantly different moralities. 'They're influenced by many things,' explains Churchland. 'History is of course one, but there's also ecological conditions. So we can see that certain social practices amongst the Inuit are different from social practices amongst people who are living in Polynesia and that's at least partly owing to the fact that life is really, really, really hard in the Arctic.'

The clearest example of this is the Inuit's strong intolerance of deception. 'Once you understand the culture a little more deeply you can see that deception really jeopardises the group as a whole, because they're always on the knife-edge of survival. Starvation is always just a seal away. So when someone deceives them about something and the whole group undertakes an activity as a result, they waste precious energy and resources. And starvation did of course happen.' There is nothing different in the 'moral brains' of Polynesians, but because in their society the challenges are different 'for them, well, you know, [deception] is a kind of a misdemeanour – you don't do that. But for an Inuit, it's very serious.'

I put it to Churchland that perhaps the most challenging feature of this account of morality is its suggestion that etiquette and morality are really on the same continuum.

'Oh, people hate that,' she says. 'Philosophers hate that.'

And the difference between the two is simply the seriousness of the situation? 'It's the seriousness, of course. It's all about social behaviour. It's all about how we get on with each other. Things like deception, murder and child neglect are very serious, whereas licking your knife or breaking wind at table, they're unpleasant but nobody suffers in an acute way.'

I suggested that an anthropologist from Mars would think that it was obvious the social and the moral were continuous because if you observe what people say about matters of supposedly pure etiquette, they use a moral language. Certain things are said to be wrong and people are called inconsiderate.

'Yes, of course. They use the same vocabulary but they don't mean it's heavily wrong. But they do punish them: they don't get invited again. They're not part of the club and they're not promoted to CEO.'

This general idea should not be seen as shocking. Nor does it in anyway debunk morality. Indeed, isn't it a non-controversial definition of morality that it concerns our duties and responsibilities to others? If we take this seriously and follow it to its logical conclusion, we can see that morality is not the opposite of pragmatism, but that pragmatism is integral to morality. Its purpose is to enable us to live together for mutual benefit, not harm. And once you accept that, you can see that justifications of all sorts of social control, punishment, blame and so forth need not rest on any deep metaphysical assumptions, but merely on what is required to keep us from each other's throats. And if that's correct, it is easy to see why concerns about free will need not be as threatening to our established morality as many have suggested.

Criminal law provides a good example of how dispensable traditional notions of free will are to the continued functioning of blame and responsibility. Churchland, for example, went looking for the concept of free will in the law and legal discussions. 'The expression "free will" never appears,' she found. 'What appears are considerations of *mens rea* [criminal intent] and whether or not there was knowledge of the conditions and so forth. Those are the things that matter, and when there is a dispute about guilt or the proper sentence the question of free will doesn't enter into it.'

Churchland is not the only person to have noticed that we don't need the traditional 'could have done otherwise' concept of free will to justify the bulk of our criminal law practices. Tamler Sommers, for example, says that 'retributive attitudes and dispositions are fitness enhancing' and that they were 'naturally selected to motivate behaviour that improves social coordination'.[21] That would mean their justification is to be found in how they regulate behaviour, not in any thoughts about ultimate responsibility. Michael Gazzaniga, the psychologist, also says that the concept of personal responsibility 'is wholly dependent on social interactions, the rules of social engagement. It is not something to be found in the brain.'[22] That means responsibility and freedom are found 'in the space between brains, in the interaction between people'.[23] That's another reason why nothing we have found out about the brain threatens what matters about free will.

In fact, the concept of responsibility might be even more detachable from that of free will, as a now famous experiment conducted by the philosopher Joshua Knobe suggests.[24] Consider this scenario. A restaurant manager wants to change his suppliers, to get better quality at a better price, and he chooses one he thinks is ideal. He runs this past his buyer who says, 'Hmm. I think you should know that this supplier has a very bad corporate social responsibility record. They have badly paid and treated workers at the end of their supply chains and environmentally damaging practices.' The manager replies, 'I don't care. I just want the best deal for us.' Should he be blamed for any of the harms caused by his supporting this irresponsible business? Hold your answer for a minute. Now imagine he makes the same proposal, but in this version, the buyer says, 'Great! That's a socially responsible company that does a lot of good for its suppliers, employees and the environment.' The manager replies, 'I don't care. I just want the best deal for us.' Should he be praised for any of the good things caused by his supporting this responsible business?

Most people blame the manager for the bad consequences in the first case but don't praise him for the good consequences in the second. The bad consequences are judged to be intentional, the good ones not. Some people believe this is inconsistent. The manager stands in the same causal relation to the effects of his actions in both cases, with the same lack of concern for them. So why hold him responsible for the bad effects but not for the good ones?

I don't think there is a puzzle here. The inconsistency only appears if you assume that the nature of the causal relationship between agent, action and consequence by itself establishes the moral status of an act. But what if the critical factor is rather simply what is required for the responsibility system to work? The manager needs to be blamed for the foreseeable bad consequences, even if he doesn't actively intend them. It's only by treating people in this way that we get accountability for bad consequences. However, there is simply no reason at all to praise people for unintentional but foreseeable good consequences. There is no benefit in terms of behaviour modification. Indeed, if anything, people should be chastised for being indifferent to the consequences. 'It's good that you're using these people, but I wish you would actively try to seek out this sort of supplier rather than just pick one by chance.' So if you're trying to do what's appropriate from a regulative point of view, the asymmetric responses to the two cases is entirely appropriate. Blame is needed, praise is not. The aim is behaviour modification, not to map an accurate metaphysics of causation.

This shows that even if determinism is true, it may still be justifiable to hold people responsible even though they could not have done otherwise. This is not as counter-intuitive as it sounds. 'One of the things that some of the experimental work has brought out,' says philosopher Shaun Nichols, 'is that even though people think that responsibility is incompatible with determinism, if you make it sufficiently vivid to them that determinism is true, they reverse that view. So if you make them think that it's actually pretty likely that determinism is true about us, then they're more likely to say that people are still responsible.'

Interestingly, he adds, that's not so true with free will. In a determinist universe, people think people would be responsible for their actions, but they wouldn't have free will. So there is a way in which even common sense can distinguish between what is required for responsibility and what is required for the traditional view of free will. 'I think that we find it pretty easy to just expunge that bit from our normal way of thinking about responsibility. There are different conceptions of responsibility, and it might be that we need to give up on a particular way that people naturally think about responsibility in favour of a regulative way of thinking about responsibility.'

To spell this out, that means we might give up the idea that to be responsible means being the ultimate originators of our actions, and to think instead that, as the very word 'responsible' suggests, it simply means to be responsive, to be able to respond to blame, praise, and so on. Responsibility in this sense is not something we just have: we can become more or less responsible, learn to take on responsibility or avoid it. And indeed we do in many ways think of everyday responsibility just like this. How responsible we take people to be depends on, for example, how old they are, how much they could reasonably be expected to know, how much in control they are. It is always a matter of degree.

Because morality is essentially rooted in the social, moral codes can reflect social mores, for better and for worse. If you look at how judgements of criminal responsibility are made, for instance, it becomes clear that social conventions are at play alongside best psychiatric evidence. Edward Rees told me that 'It's not easy to win diminished responsibility cases because it seems that juries don't like people who kill people.' Visceral hatred of killers makes it difficult for people to accept any evidence that suggests diminished responsibility.

This is particularly evident in the case of child killers, who rarely end up in Broadmoor. 'To kill a child, particularly in the context of a sexual motive, is vanishingly bizarre,' says Adshead. 'But people who kill children never come here and they never go to psychiatric services because, I think, if they come here there is some sense of feeling sorry for them and nobody's allowed to feel sorry for them.' The same is also true of people who kill their wives.

Although objectively it might seem that someone who kills a child is at least as mad as someone who kills an adult stranger, society does not tend to treat the former as ill, since that would in some sense let them off the hook, making them an object of sympathy rather than opprobrium. Although that might appear to be inconsistent, if you understand desert in terms of appropriateness, and justice in terms of a pragmatic need to regulate bad behaviour, it can make some, if not complete, sense. As Adshead said, 'Most of this is about social relations, isn't it? When somebody hurts their child, that's an offence against all of us. We all have an interest in our children not being hurt and it's an offence against the group and we want to mount a response that's fair and proportionate.'

In other ways, however, society's judgements about where to draw lines are less defensible. Generally speaking, it appears to be the case that the less sense we can make of what reasons someone might have to commit a violent crime, the more we are likely to accept that the person was insane. 'I'm afraid that's very true,' says Adshead. 'In fact there's a nice piece of research from around twenty years ago that shows that you stay longer in this place if people can't understand your offence.'

But there are some oddities about what counts as understandable. Take the man who, shortly before I met Adshead, was sentenced to thirty years for killing his wife and her child. 'He had a psychiatric report, possibly even two, that said that he was mentally ill,' said Adshead. 'The jury didn't buy it because there was an alternative story put forward by the prosecution that she was depriving him of money in the divorce and he killed her out of spite.' As she points out, that 'doesn't explain why he killed her child and the family pet as well', but 'in the theatre that is the criminal court you put forward a story and the best story wins'. In this case, the story won because people seemed to believe that 'devotion to human profit is a kind of trumping motive', one a sane, rational person might act upon. 'This story that if you were deprived of money of course you'd be so angry that you'd kill somebody, this is just mad.'

Patricia Churchland has another example of how attributions of responsibility and sanity change with the social and political winds. 'In American law, for a while the insanity defence had two components. Either you could argue that the person did not know what he was doing, he was totally delusional [the "cognitive prong"], or that he knew what he was doing but was unable to prevent himself [the "volitional prong"]. When Hinckley shot Reagan the defence was the volitional prong. He knew what he was doing – they couldn't deny that, he planned and planned and planned. But the argument was that he couldn't prevent himself, because he was so smitten by the actress Jodie Foster, and so under this compulsion that she would love him if he did this, and he was indeed found not guilty by reason of insanity. What happened then was that the public loved Reagan and the idea that this person was not guilty by reason of insanity was intolerable. So the law in most jurisdictions was changed so that the volitional prong no longer obtains, and now it's only the cognitive prong.'

When people think of the role social life plays in our conception of free will, and how responsibility is attributed even if we cannot do other than what we do, many are tempted to take the cynical view that free will is just a myth, a philosophical nonsense, but that without widespread belief in it, society would fall apart.

It certainly does seem to be true that even people who deny free will and with it praise and blame find it very hard indeed to give up all notions of responsibility. Shaun Nichols knows this from personal experience. 'I was a hard determinist since college, and then I started thinking about the fact that I never, like, excused my wife for doing something I didn't like. I didn't think, "Oh, but she's determined".' Because the belief that we have free will is so tenacious, Nichols doesn't think we need to lie to people in order to ensure they maintain it. 'People just aren't going to change. The normal emotional and moral reactions we have are way deeper than all this theoretical speculation. Hume said basically that no amount of theoretical worrying is going to displace your natural moral sentiments.'

Some go further than accepting that belief in free will is hard to shake off and claim that it would actually be bad to get rid of it, even though it is false. In this vein, the psychologist Daniel Wegner says the 'illusions piled atop apparent mental causation', of which free will is one, 'are the building blocks of human psychology and social life'.[25] Similarly, Saul Smilanksy advocates a view called 'illusionism', which maintains that 'we cannot live with complete awareness of the truth of the free-will problem, and it would be dangerous to try to do so'. The implications of this are stark: 'To put it bluntly: People, as a rule, ought not to be fully aware of the ultimate inevitability of what they have done, for this will affect the way in which they hold themselves responsible,' for the worse.[26]

Society may indeed fall apart without belief in free will, but that does not mean the only or best reason to believe in it is to hold society together. Civilisation would collapse without many true beliefs, such as that plants grow from seeds, or that we need to drink water to survive. The fact that there are social functions to morality, blame and responsibility does not show that this is all there is to them.

Fortunately, however, we don't have to agonise over the ethics of propagating a noble lie. You only have to take seriously the idea that free will is a necessary fiction if you are first persuaded that it is a fiction at all, which I am not. We have something deserving the name of free will just as long as there is a meaningful sense in which we are in control of what we think and do, and I think it should now be clear that there is. Throughout the discussion so far, there has been a stress on the fact that whether or not people have ultimate responsibility for their actions, and whether or not they could do otherwise, there is a sense in which people can regulate their own behaviour and exercise self-control. This capacity, rather than a traditional, free-floating freedom of the will, is all we need to preserve blame, praise and responsibility.

You don't need any specific scientific evidence to show that we have such a capacity. Some people can control their anger better than others, for example, and you can even be trained to improve in this respect. Nor is there anything debunking about research that shows, for example, that people are more likely to lose their temper when hungry or angry. All that shows is that our capacity to self-regulate is far from absolute and can be diminished by environmental or biological factors. Such research can help us to increase our self-control: by becoming aware of how much we are affected by food, for example, we can plan our eating to avoid glucose deficiency undermining our decision-making capacities.

This is something even arch-critic of free will Sam Harris acknowledges. 'Becoming sensitive to the background causes of one's thoughts and feelings can – paradoxically – allow for greater creative control over one's life,' he says. 'It is one thing to bicker with your wife because you are in a bad mood; it is another to realise that your mood and behaviour has been caused by low blood sugar. This understanding reveals you to be a biochemical puppet, of course, but it also allows you to grab hold of one of your strings: a bite of food may be all that your personality requires. Getting behind our conscious thoughts and feelings can allow us to steer a more intelligent course through our lives (while knowing, of course, that we are ultimately being steered).'[27]

What is telling about these remarks are the caveats Harris inserts, on both occasions accompanied by a knowing 'of course'. Harris wants to accept both that we can increase our self-control and so guide ourselves or pull our own strings; and that, ultimately, we have no control whatsoever. But this leads to paradox: puppets who pull their own strings, steerers who are themselves steered. This is unnecessary. As I have argued, ideas of 'ultimate' control are misguided. We don't need to add these caveats, at least not in the normal course of things. We can increase our self-control in all the ways that matter, and these powers do not need to be ritually denigrated because we cannot achieve the impossible and be in ultimate control.

Various definitions of human freedom over history have captured this better than some contemporary notions of free will. Michael Frede, for example, sums up the Stoic definition of freedom as 'a matter of having the ability to act on one's own, to act at one's own discretion, to act on one's own account, to act independently', while Epictetus thought it 'a matter of the will's not being prevented from making the choices it sees fit to make, of its being impossible to force it to make any choices other than it would want to make'.[28]

A similar notion is found in Hume: 'By liberty, then, we can only mean *a power of acting or not acting, according to the determinations of the will*; that is, if we choose to remain at rest, we may; if we choose to move, we also may. Now this hypothetical liberty is universally allowed to belong to every one who is not a prisoner and in chains. Here, then, is no subject of dispute.'[29]

Coming right up to date, the philosopher Manuel Vargas says: 'An agent can be said to have free will or to be acting from or with free will when that agent, in the context of deliberation or action, has the capacity to detect moral considerations and can govern him or herself [in an] appropriate way in light of these moral considerations.'[30] Similarly, John Martin Fischer bases his compatibilism on a distinction between regulative control, which requires genuine access to alternative possibilities – a strong 'could have done otherwise' condition – and guidance control, which does not. All guidance control requires is that 'the mechanism that issues in action must be the "agent's own", and that it must be appropriately "reasons-responsive"'.[31] So, for example, you had guidance control if you, rather than a computer, drove the car to your destination, and you took the route you concluded was the right one, even if you only followed a satnav. After all, if your satnav proved itself unreliable, you'd follow a different suggestion.

Tellingly, Martin Fischer says that 'the basic intuitive ideas are more important than the details', which I think is exactly right.[32]

Different philosophers formulate things in different ways, but the essential idea is clear and simple: we know there is a difference between the source of decisions and actions lying primarily within or without us. Of course there are grey areas. For instance, how much self-control does someone have when they are caught up in mass hysteria? Not as much as when they are not, for sure, but enough still to hold her responsible? There may not be a clear factual answer here, but if freedom and responsibility are matters of degree, as surely they must be, there will always be such grey areas, and no philosophy of free will that refuses to accept their existence can be remotely credible.

This is a kind of self-control that does not need to operate in isolation from the natural laws of cause and effect. Indeed, some of the most notable explanations of what self-control consists of explicitly factor in the external world. Take Kant's notion of autonomy. As the etymology suggests, this is self (*autos*) governance or rule (*nomos*, law). However, Kant did not think for one minute that this amounts to the self's capacity to make up the moral law for itself. That would not be to govern oneself according to any law but simply to act capriciously. Autonomy is only meaningful when the self directs itself according to laws that stand outside of itself.

Free will is not exactly the same, but it is analogous. A kind of self-regulation that was completely independent of nature and nurture, heredity and environment would be random and meaningless. Self-regulation only makes sense against something one can regulate oneself with.

The ways in which we foster and develop self-control show that we see the importance of external social standards. For instance, 'In the case of children,' says Churchland, 'partly what we really are concerned to do is to exploit the fact that their self-control is part of the causal nexus, and we reward them for suppressing impulses and delaying gratification and punish them for not, and so forth.' What

Churchland finds odd is that we tend to think of this as a mere training mechanism and talk as though the self-control of mature adults comes entirely from within. 'Once they reach twenty-one, we say now they're making decisions in a causal vacuum.'

Churchland sees a similar puzzle in ideas that free will is independent of physiology, since we know that 'our self-control can be compromised by being exhausted, or being highly stressed, or being terribly hungry, or by alcohol'. So 'What does one of these libertarians think happens? Is it that when I make a decision when I'm highly stressed, somehow my brain makes that decision, but when I'm not stressed, lo and behold, my free will does it? You might say you have two classes of decisions, those which are pure and those which your brain makes when you're stressed, and so forth. That's so bizarre.'

Bizarre indeed. We certainly have self-control, and it certainly is not something that exists in a causal vacuum. But is this kind of self-control what we mean by free will? It certainly may not be what some philosophers mean, which is perhaps why Churchland thinks 'the neurobiology of self-control is way more interesting than any discussion of free will in philosophy'. But perhaps the best way of looking at it is that real free will, rather than a metaphysical fantasy, is in essence 'A healthy control system where all the bits are working well – that's as good as it gets.' And that may well be more than good enough.

We clearly do have some capacity to regulate our own behaviour, yet this is not enough for many who deny free will. Why not? I think it's because we confuse two different ways of thinking about human action. Call one the metaphysical question of what ultimately *originates* our choices and behaviours. Call the other the ethical question of what essentially *regulates* behaviour. Put like that, it should be clear that these are two very different questions and the answers need not be in conflict with each other. Even if determinism is true, it clearly is the case that praise and blame, reward and punishment can change what we choose to do. That's enough for a realistic form of free will that does not require us to be originators, but merely regulators of our own behaviour.

My way of understanding responsibility requires a shift away from the past tense of 'could have done otherwise' to the future tense 'could do otherwise'. We might accept that, at the moment of action, given all that had happened in the past, a person could not have done otherwise. But we recognise that the alternative universe in which they did otherwise was not so far from the universe that actually pertained. It would not have required much more knowledge, thought, carefulness or whatever for the person to have acted differently. The point about holding them responsible is not about looking back to what is done and dusted, but looking at who they now are and making them realise that because they had all the knowledge, skills and tools available to have done otherwise, they could and should do better in future. This may seem somewhat inconsistent: blaming people for past events when the real importance is for the present and future. But this is the only way the blame system really works.

If people focus too much on the sense in which they could not have done otherwise, they feel blameless and so are unlikely to engage in the kind of self-criticism that will lead them to do better in future. We might be better off focusing less on what is done and can't be undone and more on how people move forward, although without a strong sense of having fallen short of a reasonable standard we could have attained, the required regret and remorse won't kick in.

Nonetheless, there are those who believe we really ought to do away with backward-looking notions of blame and responsibility, such as the neuroscientist David Eagleman. In his book *Incognito*, he has a chapter entitled: 'Why is Blameworthiness the Wrong Question?' When I met him, he gave me the short answer.

'By blameworthiness I mean issues about, what are all the factors that's led up to this guy right now, biological and experiential, and to what degree is it his fault versus his genetics' fault or his experience's fault? My argument is that it is absolutely an impossible question to answer, ever. That's why a backwards-looking blameworthiness is unanswerable. That's what I mean by saying it's the wrong question.'

For Eagleman, what matters is not who or what was to blame for what happened, but how we can 'rewire' the brain to stop people doing it again. Blameworthiness just isn't needed for this. 'What I'm campaigning for is a totally forward-looking system and unless I'm missing something, I don't see any flaw in running the whole system that way.'

Yet Eagleman is happy to concede that some of the best methods for rewiring the brain are good old-fashioned praise and blame, reward and punishment. 'Blame and praiseworthiness and all that stuff is exactly the kind of tool that you use moving forward,' he says, and 'I am not opposed to incarceration: it is the original rewire-the-brain strategy,' along with telling people off, spanking, fining, and so on. 'That's how you get self-regulating systems to regulate themselves better.'

It seems, therefore, that blame is only really useless in the cases where 'some people's brains, because of pathologies, aren't amenable to being modified by the traditional ways of doing it. Then it's a waste of time to make somebody bust rocks under the hot sun because you're not going to fix the problem.'

So I'm left somewhat unclear as to whether Eagleman really believes blameworthiness is always the wrong idea after all. The core of his argument is that criminal justice rests on the need to change behaviour, rather than on notions of ultimate responsibility. I agree, but don't see this as being in conflict with blameworthiness. To say someone has free will is to say that they are capable of modifying

146

their own behaviour, and that's why blame works and makes sense. To accept the blame is not to make some metaphysical claim that had history run exactly the same, then at the moment of your mistake you might have acted otherwise. It is to say that a person of your knowledge, maturity, experience and capacities could and should in a situation like that have done differently. That's the thought to focus on, and that's the thought that allows us to modify behaviour in future. To stop and ask whether, in fact, you really could have done differently on that occasion is a thought too many. And indeed, it's a thought people often have when looking for excuses.

Think back to the study by Vohs and Schooler which suggested that thinking about how actions are determined by genes and environment leads people to cheat more. Similarly, a study by Baumeister, Masicampo and DeWall suggested that 'disbelief in free will reduces helping and increases aggression', and 'serves as a cue to act on impulse, a style of response that promotes selfish and impulsive actions such as aggressing and refusing to help'.[33] Together these suggest that thinking we could not have done otherwise in the past does not help us to improve our behaviour in the future.

Gwen Adshead's front-line experiences at Broadmoor also suggest that the project of decoupling forward-looking reform from backward-looking blame is fundamentally misguided. She would agree with Eagleman that it's impossible to say whether a person really could have done otherwise in the past. 'We can't always know whether someone could have done otherwise. All that we know is that they did and at that moment they were suffused with a kind of intention to do something.' So she agrees that her main task is to enable people to do otherwise in future. To do that, you have to get people to 'relate to their minds in different ways', to be 'a bit more curious about what goes on in their minds' and to get beyond 'the idea that you have a thought and you must act on it'.

So it's not so much asking a metaphysical question of whether someone *is* responsible, but getting them to *become* more responsible, to *take* responsibility for their actions. As she explains, looking backwards is essential to this. 'When people take responsibility for things, they're relating to what they did and who they hurt in a slightly different way. There is a type of engagement with that in terms of ownership, a sense that they were there, that it is part of who they were, right then. They have to deal with that, they can't negate it, they can't deny it. And we see this in particular with people who kill.' When I met her, Adshead had been working with a depressed and psychotic man who said it was his wife's fault that she died when he killed her. 'The endgame has got to be, "I brought about her death and that was a terrible thing".'

All of this is needed if patients are to recover their sense of agency, which is essential to becoming responsible. Adshead cites the professor of criminology Shadd Maruna who has 'done some very interesting work on people who stop offending and analysing the way that they talk'. Adshead says Maruna believes 'that people who manage to stop offending talk about themselves as having more agency'. Similarly, Jonathan Adler has found that people who have a positive experience of psychotherapy tend to give a narrative of it that has more agency and coherence. 'I think there's an increasing recognition that a lot of people come into therapy in very passive states of mind, and therapy works by allowing people to take back some sense of agency and to feel not so much in control of their lives, because they might not be in control, but to have a different relationship to the way in which they experience the world, so instead of being constantly "done to" by a variety of things and people, they have more of a sense of being actors in their own narrative.'

Ironically, perhaps, psychology and therapy have historically worked against this, promoting an outmoded medical model in which people are victims, suffering from mental illnesses. 'It's been a real problem,' agrees Adshead. Today, an overzealous desire to be compassionate and understanding, often based on ideas gleaned from neuroscience that people can't be blamed for what they do, can also undermine the very sense of agency required for people to be responsible citizens.

While we should not do away with blame, I think we ought to be careful how we use it. The philosopher Hanna Pickard argues that we should avoid 'affective' blame, which involves hate, anger and resentment, and a sense that one is entitled to these negative emotions. Pickard has worked in clinical settings with people with various 'disorders of agency', such as addicts and anorexics. She has found that although it is very important for service users to be treated as responsible agents capable of making choices, it doesn't help if they are blamed in these emotionally charged ways. Hence her interest in what she calls 'responsibility without blame'. When she specifies what this is, it turns out to be responsibility without *affective* blame. This sense of responsibility still involves 'detached blame' which is 'a judgement or belief of blameworthiness' which may also lead to sanctions. But it does not feature the emotive 'sting' of affective blame.[34]

Pickard has identified something very important here. It may be, however, that there are not so much two kinds of blame, but one, which can carry a more or less powerful emotional charge. Blame is often counterproductive because it is accompanied by too much anger and resentment, but it can be effective when it is used simply to make someone aware of their responsibility. Either way, it should be clear that we do not need to do away with blame completely in order to have an enlightened attitude towards responsibility.

That an enlightened view of free will means 'we're not really going to have any punishment any more' is, thinks philosopher Daniel Dennett, 'a very shallow thought. It doesn't follow at all. There's nothing that we've learnt from neuroscience that undercuts the foundation for both the law of contract and the criminal law.'

Nonetheless, Dennett sees various versions of that radical idea out there, all of them 'hugely overdrawn'. 'If the law ever did presuppose anything like a libertarian notion of free will then it should jettison that *post haste*,' he says, because that's 'obscure and panicky metaphysics' as P. F. Strawson said. But the law presupposes no such thing.

There is even a sense in which people who go around saying that punishment is not justified and responsibility is a lie are behaving irresponsibly. The risk is that it will become a self-fulfilling prophecy. Just as experiments have shown that economics students who are told that human beings are rational self-maximisers start to think and behave more selfishly, so, as we have already seen, experiments by the likes of Vohs, Schooler and Baumeister suggest that if people are told they are not responsible for their actions, they may behave more irresponsibly.

There is a deep irony here. Believing the narrative that says we have no free will, that we are puppets of hidden causes beyond our consciousness, actually causes us to change our behaviour. But that in itself demonstrates quite clearly that what we consciously believe does affect how we act. So people who embrace the idea that our conscious deliberations change nothing demonstrate precisely what they deny.

However, although nothing we have discovered makes punishment completely unjustified, I agree with Dennett when he says that 'especially in America, we should of course reform our obscene system of criminal punishment'. For some, this means a switch from a moral to a medical paradigm, seeing criminality as a sign of mental illness. For instance, although 'neurocriminologist' Adrian Raine does not deny the role of the environment in antisocial behaviour, he claims that 'repeated violent offending is a clinical disorder' and that 'violence is already viewed as a public-health problem by the World Health Organisation and the Centers for Disease Control and Prevention'.[35] The evidence for this includes findings such as: 'poor prefrontal functioning is the best-replicated correlate of antisocial and violent behaviour', and that the relationship between a low resting heart rate and antisocial behaviour is stronger than that between smoking and lung cancer.[36]

But it does not follow from this that 'treating the physical causes [of criminality] will work more quickly and effectively than repairing the complicated social factors that also contribute to criminal behaviour'.[37] As I believe should now be clear, it is one thing to accept that there are neurological and biological factors at work in behaviour, quite another to think that we should routinely treat offenders as though they are mere puppets of them. We also need to remember the old statistical adage that 'correlation is not causation'. Many people who have the supposed biological correlates of criminal behaviour are not criminals, showing that it is too simplistic to think of hormones and brain functions as straightforward causes of crime. As for the claim that 'genes give us half the answer to the question of why some of us are criminal, and others are not', we have already seen why this is a very misleading interpretation of the claimed 50 per cent heritability of criminality.[38]

That is not to say that we should rule out quasi-medical interventions as part of a strategy for reducing crime. There is good evidence, for example, that some sexual offenders can be helped to avoid reoffending when they opt for surgical castration.[39] There may indeed be other specific biological interventions that can help people control their violent or impulsive tendencies. But we have no good reason at all to think that this approach can or should replace our systems of praise, blame and punishment wholesale. Even to attempt to do so would dangerously undermine the social reinforcement needed for autonomy to flourish widely.

Simply replacing punishment with treatment looks very mis-guided. There are other ways in which we should reform the criminal justice system. To see how to do so, we need to look at what the basic justifications of punishment are.

The first is retribution, essentially a form of payback for wrongs committed. The other three main rationales usually cited are deter-rence, rehabilitation and public protection. Sometimes a fifth is added: expressing society's disapproval of a practice, whether or not that changes any behaviour or protects anyone. Edward Rees told me that this is a factor taken into account in sentencing, where judges have to think about both the protection of the public and also how 'to mark the seriousness of the offence, and seriousness is defined by statute as involving the level of criminality plus the con-sequences of the act'. As the *Magistrates' Court Sentencing Guidelines* puts it, 'When considering the seriousness of any offence, the court must consider the offender's culpability in committing the offence and any harm which the offence caused, was intended to cause, or might foreseeably have caused.'[40]

What's interesting to note here is that of these justifications for punishment, only retribution involves any sense of responsibility. Even if we think that no one is responsible for criminal actions, forms of punishment that protect, deter, rehabilitate or send a signal would still be warranted. Each of these is a means to an end. Retribution alone requires responsibility in order to make sense.

Take retribution out of the picture, and there is both a clear rationale for criminal punishment but also a strong argument for its reform. 'At the moment I think that the sentencing system has moved a long way from clear notions of what amounts to a proper and efficient sentence,' says Rees. 'My submission would be that a sentence is only justifiable if it has some proven or likely efficacy involving protection of the public and/or reform. The sentences that are being dished out now do not meet that test. One test that you can apply is the reconviction rate.' In the UK nearly half of all prisoners released each year reoffend within twelve months.[41] 'If you took a scientific process or a business model and it had an eighty per cent failure rate, you would say this is not the right thing to do.' The only explanation for why we persist with this inefficiency is that criminal justice policy is 'politically driven'.

But is there any justification at all for retributive punishment? Of course, people who simply deny that we have free will deny the legitimacy of retribution outright. Derk Pereboom echoes the consensus view here when he says, 'If hard incompatibilism is true, a retributivist justification for criminal punishment is unavailable.'[42] The only concession that could be made to retribution is the one floated by Sam Harris, who says that 'it may be that a sham form of retribution would still be moral – even necessary – if it led people to behave better than they otherwise would'.[43]

Even if you don't go so far as to deny free will altogether, the retributive case for punishment can seem somewhat weak. Once we accept the huge role of luck, both genetic and environmental, in what we become, it is more difficult to see the justification for punishing people simply as payback. I have tried to make sense of the idea of desert in such a way that it does not imply that a person could have done otherwise at the moment of choice, but retribution does seem to rest on the stronger sense of desert which holds that a person really could have done otherwise and so must pay the price for not doing so.

However, if you take away retribution, then it seems punishment loses any connection with responsibility. We can deter, rehabilitate, protect the public and express society's disapproval without any need to blame the person we are punishing to achieve these goals. But if I am right and we each have a sense of responsibility that needs to be nurtured, that means such a blame-free criminal justice system would dispense with one of the most important factors in the self-regulation of behaviour.

My suggestion is therefore that the fourfold division between retribution, deterrence, rehabilitation and protection needs rethinking. In breaking down the justification for punishment into these four elements, something is lost in the reduction. Responsibility is filed entirely under the one element that it is hardest to defend. What is lost is the importance of bolstering and nourishing the responsibility system in individuals. It is not just about providing the incentives to deter people from reoffending or committing crimes in the first place. It is about getting people to recognise the extent to which they can be effective self-regulators, and to consider the effects their actions have on others.

To do this, it seems to me that you need to retain at least some trace of the retributive. You cannot become maximally responsible if you focus on the sense in which you could not have done otherwise or are not ultimately responsible for your actions. Responsibility is built by accepting that even though we are not entirely responsible for what we do, no seriously wrong deed can go unpunished.

Given its reputation for venality, the British Parliament provides a useful historic example of how embracing a responsibility that is not entirely yours works. It used to be accepted that if a serious mistake or a poor decision was made in a government department, the minister in charge would resign, even if he or she was not personally responsible. This was the convention of ministerial responsibility, and it held up until the mid-1980s. People used to believe that this was good and honourable. Over time, people have come to see it as somewhat bizarre, and now the convention has changed. Ministers are only held responsible for what they have personal control over.

It is far from obvious that the erosion of ministerial responsibility represents an advance. Even though on paper the old system applied too demanding a notion of responsibility, the overall effect was that judgements started with an assumption of responsibility, which would only be overridden in extraordinary circumstances.

This created a responsibility-taking culture. Now the onus of proof is on those who wish to claim that the minister had direct control over the outcome. This may seem fairer, but it fosters a responsibility-shirking culture.

In a similar way, more liberal thinking about criminal justice has all but removed responsibility from the arena. This has encouraged us to think of all the circumstances that contributed to a wrongdoing rather than our own responsibility. This reflects a wider societal shift from responsibility-taking to responsibility-shirking.

We need to reintroduce a retributive element to a progressive justification for punishment. Indeed, if we look carefully, we might find this between the cracks of the apparently purely instrumental justifications. The most effective way to deter is not simply to have a big stick and incite fear, but to make people want not to do wrong by increasing their sense of moral responsibility. Similarly, to rehabilitate, we need to learn to take full responsibility for our actions. And one of the signals punishment should send out is not just that society abhors the crime, but that it expects people to be effective self-regulators. In each case, forward-looking responsibility is built only by getting people to take responsibility for what they did in the past. To do that, you need some form of retribution, a principle that if you do wrong, there is a price to pay, irrespective of what direct benefits to you or society paying that price will bring.

Retribution has become such a dirty word in liberal circles that it is hard to make people see that it might have any value at all. But it only makes sense to dispense with it if you reject free will and deny that we have any responsibility for our actions. As long as you accept that responsibility is a matter of degree and that an ordinarily competent adult has some of it, it makes perfect sense to turn around and say 'you did wrong, now you have to pay the price', just as long as that price is proportionate. Retribution need not be hot-blooded, gratuitous revenge. Retribution can be mild, sober and just one part of the rationale for punishment. But unless we are prepared to hold people responsible for their actions, not just to deter or to rehabilitate, we are failing to treat people as having the potential for self-regulation that they do have.

The aim of the criminal justice system ought to be to enable members of society to make good decisions using their own internal resources of reflection and self-regulation. This means both providing the incentives for those without criminal records to do so, and to help those who have committed crimes not to do so again. There is a small number of criminals who are not capable of taking on responsibility, and it is futile to deal with them as though they could. But for the majority, we have to treat them as capable of exercising their freedom in order to turn their potentiality into actuality, and we can't do this if we make too much of the 'could not have done otherwise' argument. Indeed, we need to change how we understand this idea anyway. The thought that someone could have done otherwise should not be taken as a judgement about what was actually possible at the moment of decision. Rather, it is a statement about what a person could have been capable of doing in that kind of situation, given their existing capabilities and knowledge. Hence the real point of thinking 'I could have done otherwise' is 'I could do otherwise in similar future situations'. The idea that we can act other than how we do thus concerns present and future choices more than it does past ones.

We do have a responsibility system, in both social and neural senses. As philosopher Manuel Vargas puts it, this 'aims to get creatures like us to better attend to what moral considerations there are and to appropriately govern our conduct in light of what moral reasons these considerations generate'.[44] When this system works well, we can regulate ourselves, and so be as free as is required for us to be held accountable for what we do.

7

The Addict

Ask someone for an example of loss of free will and the chances are they will say addiction. Everything about the received idea of an addict points to someone with a loss of free will, when it comes to the object of their addiction. The addict 'cannot help himself', is 'compelled' to do whatever he is addicted to doing and 'can't say no'. If free will is the ability to choose one action rather than another, the addict doesn't have it.

As anyone with any up-close experience of addiction will know, however, this is far too simplistic. Addiction is an impairment of free will but it is not a complete loss of it. Understanding what is going on when a person is said to be addicted is a good way of understanding just what free will is and what hinders its fullest expression.

Fergus was a DJ who, like many in the music business, was a long-term user of numerous substances. 'Apart from crack and heroin, we were taking everything,' he told me over nothing stronger than a coffee. Now clean, he can look back at a time when he was addicted not so much to any particular drug but to 'the whole thing': the hedonistic, druggy DJ lifestyle. Which particular substance was being used on any given day didn't really matter, as long as one was, although the constant was marijuana. 'To the extent that I felt permanently compelled to smoke weed, even if on some level I didn't want to, I'd say it inhibited my freedom,' he told me. But that is not the same as saying he had completely lost all his free will. Addictions of almost all kinds leave most of a person's decision-making capacities intact. In Fergus's case, this was evident in the fact that 'I was still making choices. I managed to get through two degrees, be self-employed, release two records, DJ in Japan.'

Fergus's description of his freedom as 'inhibited' was echoed in the words of Peter, an alcoholic lecturer, who told me: 'I would say my freedom was compromised. It wasn't absent.' Later he used the term 'impaired'. These two testimonies reinforce the idea that free will is not something we do or do not have, but is a matter of degree. Addiction decreases our free will; it does not remove it.

But doesn't the very idea of addiction imply that addicts have literally no choice and are in the grip of some compulsion? No. Even though 'compulsion' is commonly assumed to be at the heart of addiction, the word does not actually appear in the world's leading psychiatric diagnostic manual. In *DSM-5*, the American Psychiatric Association's latest *Diagnostic Statistical Manual of Mental Disorders*, the two categories of abuse and dependence found in previous versions have been replaced with a spectrum within the one category of disorder, a welcome development that reflects the truth that our capacity to act freely is always a matter of degree. These criteria talk of 'taking the substance in larger amounts or for longer than you meant to', 'wanting to cut down or stop using the substance but not managing to', 'spending a lot of time getting, using, or recovering from use of the substance', 'cravings and urges', developing tolerance and withdrawal symptoms, as well as several ways in which people continue to use despite the problems that creates. You do not need to meet all the criteria to be diagnosed; rather, how serious your addiction is will depend on how many of the boxes you tick. But none of these criteria includes compulsion.

If addiction is not a compulsion, then it would seem to involve some element of choice. This suggestion offends and angers some, who take it to imply that they are entirely to blame for their predicament and that all they need do is make a bit of an effort to escape it. But that does not follow. Quite clearly, the addict's ability to choose well is severely compromised and it is not straightforward for the addict to make the right choice. To say it is a choice is not to say it is one that he could easily make. If you accept that free will is a matter of degree, there should be no problem in seeing the addict as someone who has a much-reduced capacity to choose without saying that he literally has no choice at all. In fact, as Hanna Pickard argues, 'if clinicians give up the belief that [addiction] service users have choice and control over their behaviour, they cannot rationally decide to work with service users to engage this dual capacity. Indeed, if service users themselves come to believe that they genuinely have no choice or control over their behaviour, they cannot rationally decide to try to change. For one cannot rationally resolve to change that which one believes one is powerless to change.'[1]

This might appear to be contradicted by the twelve-step recovery programme of Alcoholics Anonymous, in which the first step asks users to accept that they are 'powerless over alcohol'. Even this, however, is not as complete an admission of impotence as it seems. It is followed by an acceptance that 'a Power greater than ourselves could restore us to sanity'. In other words, it asks addicts to see that the power they need resides outside of themselves, and so they are not actually powerless if they draw upon it. And to do that, they have to make a choice: 'a decision to turn our will and our lives over to the care of God as we understood Him'.[2]

'It felt like a choice, but a choice it was very difficult not to make,' is how Peter put it. The fact that drinking was a choice is shown by the fact that there were times when he made the decision not to drink because 'I had to do some work or be somewhere'. So the language of compulsion just doesn't ring true for him. 'I didn't think I was compelled to drink, in a philosophical sense.' Rather, 'It was very difficult. I felt that not drinking was not a serious option.' If anything was inescapable, it was not drinking, but wanting to drink. 'Looking back, it was just a constant preoccupation, where the next drink was coming from.' But this inability to command our desires is just an extreme version of what we all experience. We cannot easily control what we want, but we can decide to act on those wants or not. The addict's capacity to do this is diminished, but not entirely absent.

If addicts do retain some power to choose, why then do they continue with their destructive behaviour? The unsympathetic might say they either don't want to stop or they are not trying hard enough to do so. We'll come to the question of wanting to change shortly, but first we need to consider the possibility that it's a question of application: all addicts lack is willpower.

The main problem with this idea is that it often assumes 'willpower' is a capacity we all have, albeit some more than others. This 'folk notion' of a 'kind of force', as the leading expert on the psychology of willpower Roy Baumeister puts it, is seen as 'some inner equivalent to the steam powering the Industrial Revolution'.[3] Willpower is actually not a simple force and it is not one thing at all, but a complex collection of capacities. Baumeister sees it in general terms as the ability to exercise self-control consciously. He then breaks this down into four broad categories. First, the ability to control thoughts: for instance, to avoid your mind wandering, or rumination. Second, the ability to control your emotions: to shake off anger or cheer yourself up. Third is impulse control, to resist the freshly baked cookie or turn down another drink. Fourth, there is performance control, keeping focused on the task in hand and not being distracted or unsettled by pressure.[4]

Behind all these capacities is no simple 'strength of will'. Someone's willpower might be strong in some categories, weak in others. More importantly, developing your willpower is not a just matter of trying harder, which is what addicts are often accused of not doing. It is rather a matter of knowing the right strategies to use. We can control our emotions better, for example, if we develop the ability to distance ourselves from them, as though observing ourselves from the outside. We can resist temptations more if we have a settled, unambiguous opinion about why we want to do so. Willpower is also helped if we use findings in experimental psychology to understand how our brains and bodies can help or hinder it. If we do that, we will see how blood sugar levels matter much more in this respect than the simple intention to try harder. Mental efforts also leave us depleted, so we need to make sure we don't use up cognitive energy trying to control one aspect of our behaviour if we know we're going to have to control another, more important one soon. So don't try to give up smoking and force yourself to go to the gym at the same time – make progress on one before moving on to the other.

So although it would be crass to suggest that addicts are just not trying *hard* enough, there is a sense in which many don't try *smart* enough. There are strategies you can use to make giving up easier, should you wish to, and many people don't use them, continuing to hang around with friends who drink or putting themselves in situations where smoking is a temptation. 'Not trying enough things' is a perfectly reasonable sense of 'not trying hard enough', but I suspect this is not what people usually mean. Rather, they think there is something called willpower, which we choose to exert or not. But free will involves the ability to exercise self-control consciously; it does not imply that we have a mysterious thing called a 'will', which is unfettered.

The idea that we possess some part or thing called 'the will' which performs 'acts of willing' or 'volitions' is perhaps surprisingly common. It is almost as though thinkers have systemically mistaken a figure of speech for something literal. You can see this in Schopenhauer, for example, who wrote: 'If a person wills, then he must will something: his act of will is always directed towards an object . . .'[5] Gilbert Ryle argued that this way of talking betrays a mechanistic view of human behaviour in which an inner ghost sets off motions in the physical machine. Volitions in this sense initiate chains of reaction that end in bodily movements. But to say we did something voluntarily is simply to say something about how we did it, free from coercion, because we wanted to. It is not to say that the action started with a special act of willing. Indeed, it's hard to see why anyone would think voluntary action worked like that when you only need to observe your own behaviour to see that we never consciously perform of any 'acts of will' that precede our actions. That is why, Ryle argues, when we talk of what people do we say '"He did it" and not "He did or underwent something else which caused it".'[6]

A different reason why there cannot be an independent faculty of will which either exerts itself or does not is that at root, the meaning of 'to will' in this sense is the same as 'to want'. And in the same way that you can't readily turn your wants up or down, on or off, neither can you easily intensify or weaken your will. You can only will what you want, and what you want is not easily changed.

And so although the addiction sceptics are wrong to say that addicts aren't trying enough, they are actually right when they say they often don't want to give up enough. They may insist they do, but the failure to give up almost always betrays some kind of ambivalence. Our desires are not always neatly in harmony with each other. They often compete. The addict is a chronic case of someone whose desires do not form a harmonious whole. Part of them may deeply want to quit, but another part really wants to keep using. There is an important difference between a judgement and an all-things-considered judgement, one that, shortly, we'll look at more closely.

One reason why addicts want to keep using should not be mysterious: they enjoy it. Fergus started smoking pot when he was thirteen, 'immediately enjoyed it' and became 'an enthusiastic user' for years. He looks back at his druggy past and insists: 'It was great. We all had a blast.'

Peter says the reason people drink is 'so obvious people miss it'. 'Ask any drinker, honestly, why do you drink, they might start by saying, "because I was abused as a child", or "because I was depressed". All these stories are given as though the implication would be, "until I've uncovered and solved the causes of my drinking, I've got to carry on drinking". The true answer is, "I drank for pleasure". The reason why it's difficult to stop drinking is that we do it for pleasure. It's bloody good.'

Peter and Fergus are right, but there is a complication. For years, psychologists believed that wanting and liking were basically the same thing, and that both were governed by dopamine systems in the brain. Then in 1998 Kent Berridge and Terry Robinson published a research paper that would become one of the most cited in history.[7] In it, they argued that wanting and liking were not the same at all, and that they could sometimes become very out of kilter. Addiction is the most striking example of this. Addictive substances stimulate the wanting system more and more even when they give pleasure less and less. That's why, as the psychologist Frederick Toates put it, 'Drugs like nicotine create wants that aren't matched by wanting the want.'[8]

That's why not all addicts are like Fergus and Peter. Some cease to get any significant pleasure from the substances they are addicted to. Nor do those who continue using do so *just* because they enjoy it. Clearly motivations are more complicated than that. But to ignore the role of pleasure altogether would be perverse, when this is precisely what attracts people to substances in the first place.

What's really puzzling, however, is why addicts continue to indulge their pleasure or give in to their wanting when it is so clear from the outside that the price paid is too high. The solution to this will also provide a key to understanding what free will is and why it is defective in addicts. And it comes not from an addict or a psychologist, but from an American philosophy professor.

Harry Frankfurt was not thinking about addiction when he first stumbled upon the idea that was to make his professional name. He wasn't even terribly interested in free will. But as he now tells it to me, sitting in his office one day he became 'vaguely concerned with a well-known saying from somewhere in the nineteenth century that "man can do what he wants but can't want what he wants". And it suddenly occurred to me that that's wrong. Of course you can want what you want. Maybe you can't bring it about that you want what you want, but there certainly are circumstances in which what you want is what you want to want, and circumstances in which what you want is what you wish you didn't want.'

In time this distinction would be formalised with the concepts of first- and second-order wants and desires. First-order desires are the simple desires we just have: we want a piece of cake, that dress, to go to the beach. But it is also surely true that we have second-order desires, wants about wants. The dieter wants the cake but wishes he didn't; a woman might want a smaller nose but also wish she wasn't so concerned about looking pretty; you might want to be free of your desire to go to the beach so you can get on with the work you really want to do.

Frankfurt is keen to stress that he is 'not a psychologist', and as he says in his famous paper outlining his theory, 'people are generally far more complicated than my sketchy account of the structure of a person's will may suggest'.[9] He agrees with me that if you really looked at our desires and wants and how they work, they wouldn't fit neatly into two levels. It's more multi-dimensional: we have sub-conscious desires, conflicting desires, beliefs about beliefs. His is just a kind of model to enable us to get a grip on the more basic fact that, however complicated the reality is, we have thoughts about thoughts, desires about desires, and so forth.

One complication, for example, is that people's 'desires are very fluid. What they want at one time is not what they may want a few moments later, although they might not be aware of that. They may think that they want something that they did want and now they don't want it, but they're not aware that they no longer want it. So the relationship between first-order, second-order and higher-order desires is elusive because it's often not clear what it is that a person's first-order or second-order desires are.'

Fergus, for example, tells me about when he found out that his father had two months to live. 'I remember thinking, "Shit, these next few months I have to make sure that I'm clear in the head mentally, I have to make sure that I'm not cloudy." It didn't make a difference.' He just carried on smoking dope. What seemed like a strong, settled desire to stop was no such thing.

So the strengths, natures of and relationships between our desires are very complicated. The central argument Frankfurt made is that to have a free will is no more than for your first- and second-order desires to be in harmony and for you to be able to act on them. 'What really counts is whether you have the will that you want, whether you're the person you want to be, whether in your actions you're acting as you would wish to act and that wish is one which you are glad to have. It's a lack of conflict within the self; it's a kind of harmonious organisation of the self in which there is no conflict between what I call the first orders and the second orders or the higher orders.'

In this definition, it simply isn't important whether in some ultimate sense you could not have done otherwise or that you are not
the originator of your own desires. 'It doesn't really make any difference how you came about what you want, how you came about
wanting to want something. The fact is that if you do want it, and
if that desire is one which you want to have, then that's all that could
be expected, that's all you could care about in estimating whether a
person is responsible for what he's doing or not. If he's wholeheart-
edly behind it then he's responsible for it.'

I'm not entirely convinced that it doesn't matter at all how we
acquired our desires, just as long as we now endorse them. Wouldn't
it make a difference, for example, if you found out you only wanted
to want to visit Australia because some clandestine branch of the
Australian Tourist Board had surreptitiously brainwashed you in an
extremely thorough way?

Having said that, how we acquired our desires may matter much
less than we might assume. I'm reminded of Paul Verhoeven's film
Total Recall, a version of the Philip K. Dick short story 'We Can
Remember It For You Wholesale'. In the film, the hero, Quaid, discovers that he is not the construction worker he believes himself to
be, but is a secret agent whose mind has been reprogrammed by the
authorities so that he can fulfil a dangerous mission for them. His
whole identity is a complete fiction. When Quaid discovers this he
is somewhat put out, to say the least. Both he and the viewer are left
confused as to who the 'real' Quaid is. In true Frankfurtian style, he
then reflects on the values he has come to hold since acquiring his
new identity and decides to embrace them. Although the origin of
his beliefs and values is entirely external – the messy result of self-
interested manipulation by others – he takes them as his own and
from that moment sides with the rebels under his own free will.

While the film is total fantasy, this is psychologically completely
plausible. And like all the best science fiction, in some senses it is

merely an exaggerated version of the ordinary human condition. At
some point in our lives each of us should realise that our personalities and values are not entirely of our own making. Like Quaid, we
are the product of pasts we did not shape. Yet we too can live as free
agents, so long as we want our wants, value our values and so do
what we want to want to do.

All of this reinforces a central part of my defence of real freedom:
that you don't have to be ultimately responsible for acquiring the will
that you want in the first place. Frankfurt provides the positive corol-
lary of this: you're free if you have the will that you want, and you
don't necessarily have to be responsible for how you acquired it in
order to be responsible for what you do as a consequence of it.

There is more evidence for this in some of Frankfurt's other
writing, which does not appear to be about free will and responsibility at all. He writes about caring, saying, 'when a person cares
about something, he's willingly committed to his desire. It's a desire
with which a person identifies himself.' That's another example of
the second and first orders working together, irrespective of where
those cares originally came from. Similarly, he writes about love, and
it's clear that no one would think that to say you freely love is to say
you are responsible for coming to love something in the first place.
The fact that in a very strong sense we don't choose whom we love
does not mean that we don't love freely. To love freely is simply to
endorse that love and act on it, because you want to rather than
because you feel you ought to.

To my surprise, when I asked Frankfurt if he realised his writings on love hit upon a subject that actually made his earlier points
about free will more compelling, he replied, 'Well, to tell you the
truth, I've never thought of that before. You may be right about it
now that I've had five seconds to think about it.' It's another example of the mysteries of creativity: the ideas we freely come up with
can surprise even ourselves.

All this lends further support to another idea we have already encountered: that an element of compulsion is part of what it means to be free, not an obstacle to it at all. Frankfurt provides an interesting way into this concept through the ideas of the seventeenth-century Dutch philosopher Spinoza. Spinoza is famous for his determinism, arguing that everything happens out of complete necessity. An idiosyncratic aspect of his determinism is his idea of 'god-or-nature', in which he sees the two things as synonymous. Spinoza's God is both completely free and completely necessary. How can this be so?

First of all, it is not such an eccentric view that God embodies a kind of necessity. The ontological argument for the existence of God, which has recurred in many versions in Christian and Islamic theology, postulates him as a necessary being, one who must exist. What is more, since God is all-knowing and all-loving, there is a sense in which he necessarily does what is best. That's why Pierre Bayle in his *Dictionnaire historique et critique* argued that God created the world by the necessity of his own nature, not by an act of free will. At the time, however, this was heretical and he was called an atheist for his pains.

God's freedom is not therefore a freedom to do otherwise. God could not decree that thou shalt murder, as to do so would be contrary to his nature. God's freedom is rather the freedom to act solely according to his nature, with unlimited power to do so. 'God does not act from freedom of will,' wrote Spinoza. 'Things could not have been produced by God in any other way or in any other order than is the case.'[10] That is not the denial of freedom, but an affirmation of its purest essence. 'That thing is said to be free which exists solely from the necessity of its nature, and is determined to action by itself alone.'[11]

Freedom can thus be understood as the capacity to live and act entirely according to your true nature, while the absence of freedom is to live contrary to it. That's why, as Frankfurt explains, 'there's a substantial tradition in philosophy, and theology also, of asserting that submission to the will of God is true freedom, and that's not only true freedom, it's the highest freedom, the most complete freedom.' 'Submission' doesn't sound like freedom, but the idea is that only by doing this do we realise our full nature as God's creatures.

If that example is too theistic for agnostics and unbelievers, there are other examples where freedom appears to require necessity. 'One of the instances in which I think that this notion of necessity and freedom is illustrated in familiar life,' says Frankfurt, 'is when you see or grasp a proof and recognise that the conclusion necessarily follows from the premises. There's a kind of liberation in that. You feel somehow that you escape from doubt; the necessity relieves you of the burden of equivocation, the burden of ambivalence. Now you know what you really think and you are absolutely confident of your thinking.'

It's like Orwell's line in *1984*: 'Freedom is the freedom to say that two plus two make four.' At first sight, this seems odd, since 2 + 2 = 4 is as clear an example of a necessary truth as you could find. But the liberty to assert falsehoods capriciously would be a hollow freedom. To be free requires the ability to understand what is true and willingly submit to it. In that sense, philosophy is the free pursuit of unfreedom. We are looking not to create but to discover, to find what truth demands. When an argument seems right, we have no choice but to assent to it. A good argument is one we have to accept, not one we choose to endorse. Although we undertake philosophy freely, what we are looking for are arguments that we find we have to accept. More broadly, we often feel least free, least in control of our own actions, precisely at those times when choices are hard because the right decision just isn't clear and nothing is pushing us one way or the other.

Even when there is no strict necessity, many of the things we most value are precisely of the sort that most centrally involve a kind of submission to something beyond voluntary control which may be indifferent to our other desires, such as rationality and loving, things which people feel are sources of freedom but are absolutely about submission.

In one respect, this does run counter to the way we ordinarily think about free will. 'Sometimes when people talk about free will what they have in mind is the escape from necessity, that I can make a difference in the world regardless of what came before, regardless of what I've been conditioned to do,' says Frankfurt. 'I have a free will, I can sort of opt out of the course of nature and impose my will.' That notion doesn't add up, as we've seen. But there is another 'concern of people who are concerned with free will', which is 'having the will I want to have, being the person I want to be. Not so much that I am the ultimate origin of what I am. I'm not the first cause of my nature or of my will or of my desires, but that's OK as long as they're mine, as long as I take responsibility for them. What I think counts is not so much being responsible in the causal sense, but taking responsibility, in the sense in which I identify with these feelings, I accept them as my own.'

In some contexts, not being the originator of our beliefs and values gives them even more power. If you think back to how political dissidents are committed to their values, or how people will die for their religion, what moves them is not something they just happen to have chosen, it's something that imposes itself on them. Frankfurt agrees, adding, 'It's not so much that it just happens to come to them; it fits in, in an integral way, with what they are.'

Frankfurt's model perfectly captures the plight of the addict. In Frankfurt's terms, the addict's free will is compromised because there are conflicts between his desires, tensions between the things that he wants, and between those wants and the wants he, on reflection, would like to have. That certainly fits the experience of the addicts I spoke to.

'Very, very slowly, over the years, for whatever reason, I would say that I was disposed to choose to drink to excess on the basis of dysfunctional desires,' says Peter. Not that his excessive drinking wasn't initially entirely a matter of free choice. 'In a strange sense, I wasn't acting against my will. I was choosing to drink to excess because I liked it, and eventually because it became very uncomfortable not to.' When drinking started to create real problems, tensions between his first- and second-order desires started to arise. 'It's certainly true that if I could have taken a pill that would have stopped me wanting to drink beyond the point when it was just nice and sociable, then I would have done so.'

By this point, Peter 'knew my desires were disordered and very destructive and I very often wished I didn't have them. I had second-order desires very much against those, but I suppose they weren't so much against those to stop them. So I felt I was choosing to indulge this addiction while wishing I didn't want to. I knew I was acting against a lot of the things I valued in life like getting on with my career, forming a relationship, being a useful member of society.' But these desires were competing with other, more immediate, powerful ones. 'There was still this very attractive comfort of this very attractive buzz. You see, the thing is, it's very pleasant. If you meet a lot of alcoholics, as I have done, you basically find people who say it was all a nightmare. No it wasn't. The highs are pretty good.'

Fergus too noticed that his desires were not keeping step with each other. 'One of the reasons why it became problematic is because I started to realise that the whole thing was addictive and it was becoming out of kilter with the way I wanted my life to go.'

For both Peter and Fergus, being able to stop has required narrowing this gap, even if it can't be completely closed. This requires coming to an all-things-considered judgement that, if not fully endorsed by both first- and second-order desires, then at least permits a working truce between them. As Fergus put it, you need to become clear about 'the wants that you no longer want', but 'before that, there's a time when you're more ambivalent about it', and that means there isn't the resolution to actually stop.

Although for Fergus 'the all-things-considered judgement started to weigh in favour of not doing it as time went on', why did it finally do so? What made the change for him, and for Peter, that enabled a harmony of desires to arise?

The answer does not seem to involve any application of willpower. 'What is so weird about it is that for years and years I was like, "How can I stop smoking weed?" Just trying to fight against it didn't do any good,' says Fergus. 'Then something changed psychologically and I just stopped without any effort.' For whatever reason, something in the perception of the incentives changed. Fergus has quit smoking several times, for instance, and every time 'it's required no effort, no massive application of will. Suddenly the calculation in my head goes: you've got to stop.'

Similarly, Peter found that as his alcoholism got worse, 'I would say that I did at times, particularly after drinking, feel very strongly a lack of alignment between the way I wanted my desires to be and the way they were. And I was always aware, simultaneously, that that thought alone was not enough to remove the desires, and it was very good to satisfy them.' The mental shift that has to happen for the desire to stop to turn to action 'comes from the stark recognition that you're responsible for this mess, that you are actually able to give it up, and people do. I know people who have given up on their own. They think, "I'm responsible for this, I'm morally responsible, I am not the victim of illness. But the upside is, I can change."'

It's about 'recognising autonomy', he says. 'The truth is you just have to decide you've got to change or you'll die, and you do that by recognising the addictive thoughts in you for what they are and just saying, I got to this position by making stupid choices; I can now make good choices.'

The irony is that we cannot simply choose to recognise the scope of our own autonomy. We are not free to identify the extent of our freedom at a time of our choosing. We might actually be dependent on other people and our society to realise our free will, because in a sense we have to be made aware of the extent to which we can develop our autonomy to actualise our potential freedom. As Frankfurt says, 'the environment plays a great role, not just the social environment but the natural environment as well'.

It's not difficult to think of examples where we need others to make us realise how free we actually are. Take, for instance, people who feel trapped in abusive relationships. Outsiders are baffled: why don't they just leave? But as we have seen in the case of twins Ann and Judy, for those inside it really isn't that simple. Their own feelings of inadequacy and false sense of responsibility for all that is wrong make them incapable of seeing how much power they really have. When others – if others – can make them see this, then things can rapidly change. Ann escaped quickly from her abusive marriage because her social network showed her the possibility of a way out, while Judy's environment was reinforcing her sense of impotence, with even her own mother telling her she had to lie in the bed she had made for herself. No power has been given to the person that they did not in a sense already have, but it sometimes takes outside intervention to make people see the power latent within them. Some chains keep us tied down simply because we believe they cannot be shaken off.

In other situations, political and social structures blind people to their own potential. If, for example, society decrees that a woman is not permitted to become a mathematician or prime minister, then it may be that she does not even realise that she has the abilities required to succeed in either role. Rahela Sidiqi testified to this in our discussion of political freedom earlier.

It is because we often need to be made aware of our own power to change that Peter is unenthusiastic about Alcoholics Anonymous, which insists that a key step to recovery is recognising your own powerlessness and dependence on some kind of 'higher power'.

'If you buy into programmes that tell you you have no power, that becomes self-fulfilling. Tell people they have no power and they have a wonderful excuse not to exercise the power they have. We are autonomous, or we can become so if we realise we can become so. Drinking is always a choice; relapsing is always a choice.'

Similarly, describing alcoholism as a disease can, Peter thinks, encourage thoughts of impotence. 'Many of those who say that [alcoholism is a disease] think this implies they've got no power.'

Before concluding this chapter, it's worth taking a few moments to think about an interesting coda to Frankfurt's intellectual biography. His famous first paper on free will used a thought experiment to demonstrate why it was that the inability to do otherwise does not necessarily entail a lack of free will. Many other versions of this have been developed and are known as 'Frankfurt-style cases'. Their key feature is that someone is able to intervene to make you act one way rather than another, but doesn't because it becomes clear you are going to act the way they want you to anyway. In such a situation, it is true that you could not have done otherwise, but nonetheless it also seems true that you did, as a matter of fact, act on your own free will.

To take one archetypal example: a person is unsure whether to vote Republican or Democrat. That notorious stock character from philosophical fictions, the evil genius, wants to make sure that he will choose Democrat, and she has a radio-controlled implant wired up to the voter's brain, of which he is entirely unaware. The evil genius has the power to control the neuron firing to ensure that he votes Democrat, but will only intervene if, in the polling booth, she sees that he is about to vote Republican. As it happens, the voter just decides to vote Democrat anyway and the evil genius does nothing. In such a situation, it seems clear that the voter chose freely, but it is also clear that he could not have voted otherwise: any attempt to have done so would have led to the evil genius stepping in and altering his choice. And so it seems that acting freely does not require the power to do otherwise after all. All it requires is that you act as you wanted to, without coercion or outside manipulation.

Actually, I don't think this kind of thought experiment is central to Frankfurt's argument, and I have here argued for his central claims without recourse to it. But in the philosophical literature, a whole industry has been created in which people amend and develop Frankfurt-style cases to attack or defend his conclusion. Frankfurt once told a colleague, John Martin Fischer, that this devising of ever more elaborate examples was 'a young person's sport'.[12] Is it, I asked him, a game in which the whole point of the exercise has got lost?

Frankfurt does regret 'the way in which analytic philosophy has developed into a game of dealing with the intricacies of logic and analytical relationships', and yet he doesn't want to be too critical of this 'because I am an analytic philosopher: I was trained as such and I believe in it. So I don't think that it's a waste of time to devise appropriate counter-examples to standard issues, standard discussion; nor do I think it's a waste of time to criticise those accounts. But one does get the feeling that sometimes the game gets away from you and you forget how to keep score, or you forget what the goals are, or what counts as a goal. I guess I do think that in the controversy that we're talking about, many people have lost sight of what I think of as the central idea that led me to generate that counter-example in the first place, or led me to look for that example in order to illustrate the general idea. Yeah, I do think that the thing has taken on a life of its own in which the main prize has been lost sight of.'

I mention this because I think this is true of much of the literature on free will. Debates have taken on lives of their own, and arguments end up being between competing positions, rather than about the real heart of the issue. To think clearly about free will, it is important to take note of the contributions of others, but at the same time, it is important to keep your eye on the ball and remember what the real goal is. That's why this book has not followed every contour of the contemporary philosophical debate. What really matters about free will is not always what really matters to philosophers trying to make their contribution to the very particular debate about free will in their tradition.

Peter had been dry for just ten months when I met him, and admitted he could not swear he'd never drink again. When I asked him if he felt freer now, he replied, 'Yes, as a person I do. A lot of the time I wasn't exactly intoxicated but I was sort of getting there, I was functional but not right. So I couldn't be very productive, I wasn't free to be productive in the ways I wanted to be. So I feel I'm generally freer to enact my values. As long as I stay down this course, a particular, very significant obstacle has been removed.'

Fergus had been off drugs for several years and claimed that he was channelling his addictive tendencies into more constructive activities, such as his PhD. For both him and Peter, as for all of us, the capacity to exercise their free will does not imply an absolutely perfect alignment of all their desires. Conflict remains. But it is conflict that is managed, and which does not create impossible tensions on a daily basis. The difference now is not that their destructive desires have gone, but that they know they don't have to act on them, and that other, incompatible desires matter more. That makes them more free, if not perfectly so. As Frankfurt put it, reasserting a central point of my argument: 'The situation is not that we are either free or not free, but that we are free to a certain extent.

Perhaps none of us is ever entirely free, ever achieves complete freedom, but it certainly is a matter of degree.'

The experiences of addicts like Fergus and Peter are not completely alien to the rest of us, who often feel that there are aspects of ourselves and our desires we can't control. To maximise our ability to self-regulate, we have to be very sensitive to the ways in which biology and environment diminish it. Rather than relying solely on 'willpower', which is in any case something of a fiction, we need strategies to make sure control is where we want it to be. These include not just mental discipline, but organising our environments to make sure they support, rather than work against, our all-things-considered desires. For example, there is the 'Ulysses trick' of metaphorically tying ourselves to masts, avoiding giving in to temptation by knowing what we can't resist and so making sure the resistance is done for us. So people addicted to gambling can in some jurisdictions ban themselves from entering casinos, or spendaholics can hand their bank cards to trusted others.

Addiction, like phobias, shows how freedom can be diminished to the extent that it almost appears to be absent. But it very rarely goes this far. In one more way we can see that being free is not a capacity we simply have, it is something we have to work on, to protect and to nurture.

PART FIVE

Freedom Earned

8

The Philosopher

Given that the free will debate is one of the oldest in philosophy and considered by many still to be one of the most intractable, how can I have the audacity to claim that we actually understand pretty well what it is and why it's real, as I will shortly do in the concluding chapter?

Many people who have sat down to write about free will have got up from their writing desks believing that they have finally nailed the idea. Yet the debate refuses to go away. P. F. Strawson had the wisdom to see this coming as he delivered his own attempt to settle some of the issues. 'This lecture is intended as a move towards reconciliation,' he said at the beginning of his classic 1962 essay 'Freedom and Resentment', 'so it is likely to seem wrongheaded to everyone.'[1]

Strawson is right, but claiming that free will has been mapped sufficiently well for us to find our way around it takes less chutzpah than it might seem. As I said in the introduction, it is not that I claim to have hit upon the elusive missing fact or argument that finally clinches the debate. Every piece of the puzzle I have assembled has been made by others before me.

Nonetheless, any claim that an issue can be resolved when so many think otherwise requires an explanation of why it is that the debate never ends, even as I claim that, on the most substantial points at least, we know enough to reach a satisfactory conclusion. This explanation is important for more than just the free will issue. It actually concerns the whole way in which we do philosophy, its limitations and major flaws. Philosophy may well have provided us with all the tools necessary to understand free will, but she has also kicked up such a dust that sometimes it is a wonder we can see anything clearly at all.

One barrier to resolution could be that we find it hard to shake the conviction that there is one thing called free will, which exists or does not. If the picture is more complicated than that, which it surely is, then to continue asking the question 'Do we have free will?' and expecting a yes or no answer is bound to be inconclusive: people who answer 'Yes' may simply be talking about something different from those who say 'No'.

Philosophers have their own professional variant of this weakness. One standard way of characterising the philosophical enterprise is that it aims to clear up 'aporias', groups of claims 'that are individually plausible but collectively inconsistent', as Nicholas Rescher puts it.[2] Moral dilemmas arise, for example, because it appears to be right both to treat everyone impartially and to treat your own family favourably. The problem of consciousness is that we must seemingly consider human beings to be entirely physical creatures, yet consciousness does not seem to be a property of physical matter. The goal of philosophy is to confront these contradictions and replace them with something coherent, doing justice both to the competing facts of experience and to the demands of rational consistency.

The free will debate can also be seen as an aporia, populated with the individually plausible but collectively inconsistent beliefs that nothing is the cause of itself and that we do in some meaningful sense cause our own actions; and that we are responsible for our actions but are not ultimately responsible for who we are and what we do. The problem is that when philosophers seek to remove these *aporias*, they appear inclined to do so in such a way that results in a single, unified account of what 'free will' is. This would seem to be the purest way of tidying up the conceptual mess. It is not, however, the only way to end up with a more coherent picture. The alternative strategy is not to force conflicting ideas too closely together, but rather to more carefully separate them.

Take as a simple analogy something you might eat; say, a plate of roast beef, steamed carrots, fried mushrooms and braised cabbage. We might imagine someone completely unfamiliar with western cooking being puzzled as to how one dish could at the same time be roasted, steamed, fried and braised. Knowing better, we can see that this is a comical misunderstanding. There is nothing paradoxical here because the dish has four elements, all cooked in different ways. Similarly, someone baffled to find that Christians believe both that priests should and should not be married would be easily enlightened by realising that Christians come in different forms.

Beliefs about free will are essentially the same. We are puzzled because our choices seem both chosen and determined, things we could and could not have done otherwise, the result of meaningless brain processes and meaningful thought processes. If we try to work out how all this could be true of one thing, we are going to be led to paradox and confusion. If, however, we separate out the elements of what we are talking about more clearly, we can see that free will is no more paradoxical than a roast dinner in which much is not roasted at all.

Rather than being one thing with contradictory properties, free will could then be more than one thing, or just have more than one form, each with different properties. We need to understand 'free will' as involving several different things, which, for historical reasons, have been too closely tied together. If we disentangle them, we might find that we do not have contradictions within one thing, but several different things that are consistent with each other.

The philosopher Al Mele is sympathetic to this broad way of understanding free will. He won a multimillion-dollar grant from the Templeton Foundation to run a project on free will, and as a result received a fair bit of media attention. 'People would ask me, "Does free will exist?" and right away I would ask them, what do you mean by it?' he told me. 'And if they were to ask me is what you call free will important, well, there's no one thing that I call free will because I leave it open and give people different options.'

Of the understandings of free will Mele thinks are credible, 'maybe there's no fact of the matter about which of those two is better or correct'. The philosopher's job is to 'lay out clear conceptions' and then, 'if we're interested in science, see if we can find evidence one way or the other that this thing exists'. But if someone then says 'that definition doesn't really latch onto free will', there isn't a decisive way of showing that they are right or wrong. We just have to be flexible. Whether you want to call that notion free will or not, 'it might latch onto something interesting, and we want to know whether we have it or not'.

It certainly seems that philosophical disagreements often rest at least in part on what people mean by a term. David Hume believed that the persistence of a debate was itself evidence that participants were talking at cross purposes. 'From this circumstance alone, that a controversy has been long kept on foot, and remains still undecided, we may presume that there is some ambiguity in the expression, and that the disputants affix different ideas to the terms employed in the controversy.'[3]

Does this mean that at the end of the day the debate really boils down to mere words? Does it just 'depend on what you mean by free will' and that, like Humpty Dumpty, you can mean whatever you want to mean? Not quite. When there is a choice of how you describe something, and neither description is objectively right or wrong, the question of which description is better becomes one of value. We are no longer asking what is true and what is false, but what matters most. So it is we can think of free will in different ways, and once we've clarified what each way of thinking entails, we have to decide which, if any, captures what we value, or ought to value, about human freedom. And we also have to decide whether or not the kind of freedom we have merits the label 'free will'.

My own judgement is that the kind of real freedom we have can rightly be called free will. Those who claim that free will is an illusion are overstating their case. However, as we know from ancient Greece, it also seems possible to have a robust notion of human freedom and responsibility without the modern concept of free will. This makes the notion of 'free will' an unusual one. The assertion of its existence is what I'd call a *discretionary truth*. Truth is standardly taken to be a bivalent property, meaning that a statement is true or it isn't. From this it follows that if you do not accept that something is false, unless you simply don't know what to think, you accept it is true. However, I think there is a class of statements, which, although it is wrong to say they are false, we can equally well do without asserting their truth.

The concept of 'terrorism' might provide one such example. Some have argued that 'terrorism' is an empty concept and we should just do away with it. I think this is too strong and that there is a meaningful sense of the word. Nevertheless, it is a contested one and it is perfectly possible to describe different forms of violent action in terms of the perpetrators' goals, methods, legitimacy, and so on without using the word. You can argue about the comparative morality of the bombing of military targets that results in some civilian casualties, and suicide bombing, without ever having to use the word 'terrorist' or deciding whether 'terrorism' is wrong. Because of this, 'x is a terrorist act or group' is a discretionary truth: you don't need to assert it, and it may in some ways be better to avoid using this kind of language, but to say it is false is going too far.

A much less serious example is a claim such as 'blueberries are superfruits'. The term 'superfruit' is not a particularly robust one, and many nutritionists think it's best avoided. Nonetheless, it is not completely meaningless. A superfruit is one that contains particularly high concentrations of important nutrients, and there are indeed some such fruits. So, again, although we don't need the term, and in some ways would be better off without it, saying blueberries aren't superfruits is just untrue.

As these examples show, discretionary truths concern discretionary concepts: ones that have some meaning but are not needed to make sense of the world. Free will is one such concept. To assert that 'we have no free will' is false, because there is at least one meaningful kind of free will which we do have. However, that is not to say that we need the concept of free will, or that it is even useful. Someone who says that 'free will' is too ambiguous and has too many misleading connotations may well be right. But they are not thereby saying that free will does not exist.

I sometimes find myself attracted to this view. No matter how much compatibilists insist that free will requires no magic, no unmoved mover or uncaused cause, the assumption that free will does indeed require such things stubbornly persists. Perhaps then it is better to drop the term. But on balance, I think this is unnecessary and unhelpful. To cease talking about our 'free will' would inevitably risk the appearance of actively denying it. Furthermore, I think the idea that human action is somehow free-floating and unconstrained is too pervasive for it to be got rid of by the simple act of removing the term 'free will'. So there is no short cut here. The best route forward is to continue to argue that we do have free will, but that it's just not what many, perhaps most, assume it to be.

However, because that is a discretionary truth, some will persist in exercising their discretion and refuse to endorse it.

There is a second reason why philosophy finds it hard to settle the free will debate. This is exemplified in the strange reluctance of many philosophers to fully embrace the idea that both free will and moral responsibility are not all-or-nothing. As Tamler Sommers notes, 'It is surprisingly difficult to find discussions in the philosophical literature of degrees of moral responsibility', even though I think he is right to say that the absence of such a notion from a theory of moral responsibility would be a 'serious flaw'. The real defect, however, may be deeper in the philosophical method than this.

Sommers suggests that one reason why there isn't enough consideration of degrees of responsibility could be because theories 'tend to be framed in terms of necessary and sufficient conditions'.[4] The necessary and sufficient conditions approach looks for clear criteria for the correct application of a concept. So, for example, we ask, What is knowledge? One popular definition is that to know something you must (1) believe it is true; (2) it must actually be true; and (3) you must be justified in believing it is true. None of these conditions is sufficient for knowledge by itself or even in pairs. You might believe something to be true with some justification, for example, but simply be wrong. However, each of the three conditions is necessary, as without one part of the trio, you can't have knowledge. Together, they describe the necessary and sufficient conditions for knowledge.

Many philosophers do not think this tripartite account of knowledge works, but they nonetheless approve of the goal of specifying necessary and sufficient conditions for knowledge. It is, however, an approach that is antithetical to seeing anything as a matter of 'more or less' rather than 'either/or', and could be a fundamentally misguided way of understanding how concepts work and what they mean. It's certainly true that no one learns what a concept means and how to apply it by internalising some set of criteria, such as a list of necessary and sufficient conditions. Wittgenstein famously and persuasively argued that this is because the meaning of a word is determined by the way it is used, not a formal rule. Indeed, it is precisely because we don't need formal rules for the correct application of words that philosophers can spend millennia trying to define them. In the meantime, ordinary language speakers get along just fine.

Grasping the meaning is therefore a kind of *knowing how* rather than *knowing that*. The test of comprehension is whether you can use the word accurately, not how clear a definition you can offer. Everyday experience supports this. We often find it very hard to define words that we can nonetheless correctly use. Definitions are of course extremely useful in pinning down what accurate usage requires and in teaching what words mean. But definitions describe words; they do not constitute their essence.

Wittgenstein's armchair ideas appear to have a lot in common with the empirical Prototype Theory developed by Eleanor Rosch.[5] Her basic idea is that the meanings of most words have what is called a radial structure. Imagine word meanings as represented by a fuzzy-edged circle. In the centre are the clearest, prototypical things, actions or qualities to which the word applies. These are the kinds of things we put on flashcards to teach children new words: perfect red apples, elephants with fine tusks and trunks, ships with big sails. We learn what words mean by learning that these are their prototypes. But as you get further away from these clear-cut applications, things get fuzzier, and there is a point at which it is not obvious whether the word applies or not. It's like the colour spectrum. There is a colour that is unmistakably yellow, but as you move along to longer or shorter wavelengths, it becomes less and less clear-cut whether it is still yellow. Extend the wavelength enough and it's clear it's now orange, but between the two, there just isn't a definitive answer as to which colour it is. The same basic principle applies to many other concepts. Most comfortable seats clearly fit the proto-type of 'chair' or 'sofa', but it isn't always obvious whether a wide seat is a narrow sofa. More importantly, there is no fact of the matter in such cases because there are no necessary and sufficient conditions that determine the correct application of each word.

This may seem straightforward, obvious even, but it's dynamite when applied to philosophical discourse. Patricia Churchland, for example, told me about a discussion at a conference in Munich about how to define the concept of an explanation. 'My argument was, here we have philosophers of science who have spent years and years of their lives trying to get a precise definition of what an expla-nation is, and I said: look, suppose it's like "mountain", where there is no point in defining it precisely, and any attempt to define it pre-cisely is only going to lead to all kinds of controversy and is really unproductive. So why don't we just say, explanations about natural phenomena are about trying to locate that phenomenon in the causal structure of the world. Don't worry about getting more pre-cise than that. That's good enough for what we actually need. And I think that's true of the concepts of "moral", "worthwhile" or "guilty" or "responsible", and so forth – they're all radial categories and they all have prototypes and they all have fuzzy boundaries where we don't know what to say.'

I can buy that, but needless to say, it didn't go down very well in Munich. I put it to Churchland that this is in part because philosophers are resistant to 'more or less' and 'good enough'. For them, more or less isn't good enough.

'They rear back in horror,' she agrees. 'I said, look, give me a really good example of where genuine progress has been made where something has been defined precisely within philosophy and where it's made a difference, to the law, to science, to psychology –

just give me one. Nobody can. What's the point of trying to give necessary and sufficient conditions? What everybody ends up doing is fighting over the borderline cases where there is never going to be a satisfactory answer. It's like fighting over whether parsley is a vegetable. Where is the answer? If it's not in Plato's heaven and if it's not among my English-speaking colleagues who use parsley, where is it?'

Even very good philosophers can be too much in thrall to the apparent rigour of the necessary and sufficient conditions approach. These days, Harry Frankfurt is most famous for a short essay, 'On Bullshit', which became a surprise bestseller. There he wrote, 'any suggestion about what conditions are logically both necessary and sufficient for the constitution of bullshit is bound to be somewhat arbitrary'. I couldn't agree more. And yet he then says, 'nevertheless it should be possible to say something helpful' and goes on to try to specify the necessary and sufficient conditions anyway.[6] But why would anyone want to carefully specify *arbitrary* conditions? Reviewing the book, I expressed the hope that Frankfurt was in fact parodying Anglo-American philosophy's fondness for this particular method, but if he was, he hasn't come out and said so yet.[7]

To see just how profound a challenge the rejection of the necessary and sufficient conditions approach is to philosophical orthodoxy, consider how the standard way of 'making progress' in the discipline is precisely to examine those borderline cases. For instance, take the tripartite definition of knowledge I mentioned earlier, that knowledge is justified true belief. Philosophers have tested this definition by seeing if it works for borderline cases. Unsurprisingly, they find it does not, at least not very well. For example, I might believe with justification that the person I saw enter the bar is John, because I know John, the person looks like John and indeed it is John. The three conditions of justification, truth and belief are met. But what I don't know is that John has an identical twin who entered the bar a minute earlier. Had I looked then, I would also have thought John had entered the bar and I would have been wrong. The fact that I didn't and was right a minute later is therefore a matter of luck. And what we come to believe by luck can't be knowledge, can it? And so begins the endless game of refining definitions, coming up with more counter-examples to challenge them, further refinement, and so on.

The challenge of Wittgenstein and Rosch is that this whole process of defining, providing counter-examples and refining definitions is totally wrong. As Churchland put it, 'it really is chomping at the legs of that whole superstructure of stuff where you dream up counter-examples to somebody else's. That isn't even an interesting project.' There is a saying in the legal world that hard cases make bad law, and it seems hard cases make for bad philosophy too. Trying to understand what anything means by focusing on the borderline cases is to look precisely in the wrong place, like heading to a folk festival when you're seeking out the best jazz.

Such ideas don't tend to go down well with analytic-minded philosophers. 'I feel like the bad girl of philosophy even though I'm bordering on the ancient,' says Churchland. But I think she is on the right side of this argument. That makes talk of 'responsibility' and 'freedom' even more slippery. Not only are they matters of degree, it is not even always clear whether the words apply in a given context or not. Dealing with this level of ambiguity can be frustrating, but if the alternative to authentic vagueness is bogus precision, we have no choice.

Perhaps the most fundamental reason why the free will debate never ends is that ultimately the choice is between an unrealistic, pure form of free will that some will refuse to give up, employing every tool in the philosophical box to defend; and a more realistic view of free will that many feel is a 'watered-down' version of the real thing, as Robert Kane puts it.[8] Others dismiss compatibilist accounts of free will in less temperate terms. For Sam Harris, it amounts to nothing more than the assertion: 'A puppet is free as long as he loves his strings.'[9] Kant called it a 'wretched subterfuge', James a 'quagmire of evasion' and Wallace Matson 'the most flabbergasting instance of the fallacy of changing the subject to be encountered anywhere in the complete history of sophistry'.[10] For many, the free will that compatibilism offers is never as attractive as what they set out to look for, and so we are caught between settling for what we can get or holding out for the elusive ideal.

There is no reason why the right understanding of free will is obliged to be exactly the same as the common sense one. Conceptions can evolve, and it is unreasonable to insist that if you propose any alteration you are simply changing the subject. 'Imagine a discussion with someone in the fourteenth century articulating a pre-chemical theory of water,' says Manuel Vargas. 'It would strike us as unreasonable if such a person were to declare: "Either our pre-chemical theory of water will be vindicated by natural philosophy, or we will have watered down the meaning of water!"'[11]

Vargas suggests that 'we might have free will but it might be different than we tend to suppose'.[12] Accordingly, he advocates a 'revisionist' conception of free will, which he says 'can be considered a species of compatibilism' which is 'a replacement and upgrade of commonsense'. As he wittily puts it, this 'revisionist free will is even better than the real thing, for on my view it has the comparative advantage of existing'.[13]

As I have argued, I don't think that the naive idea of pure freedom is so wonderful or desirable, and I think that real freedom is more than valuable enough. But I know that many have not been persuaded, and that won't change overnight. 'It's the story of my life,' Daniel Dennett told me when I discussed this problem with him. One of Dennett's favourite quotes is from the magician Lee Siegel, who wrote, 'I'm writing a book on magic, I explain, and I'm asked,

Real magic? By real magic people mean miracles, thaumaturgical acts, and supernatural powers. No, I answer: Conjuring tricks, not real magic. Real magic, in other words, refers to the magic that is not real, while the magic that is real, that can actually be done, is not real magic.'[14]

'For many people, if free will isn't real magic, then it's not real,' says Dennett. They will not settle for any account in which free will turns out to be plain old boring real, no more than functions of lumps of physical matter obeying the laws of physics. 'Because both free will and consciousness have been inflated in the popular imagination, and in the philosophical imagination, this is a big deal. Anybody who has a view of either one that is chopped down to size, this is, as Kant said, a "wretched subterfuge". Well, it's not the overwhelming, supercalifragilisticexpialidocious phenomenon that you thought it was, but it's still real.'

The resistance of many to what I see as realistic accounts of free will seems to me to be no more than a kind of philosophical table thumping, insisting that 'it's just not the same!'. How can it be that an account that seems sensible to many informed experts looks to others as though it completely misses the point? Philosophy has generally shied away from using personality to explain theoretical differences, but in doing so I think it has skirted over an important but embarrassing truth: no one simply goes 'wherever the wind of argument carries us', as Plato described the philosophical ideal.[15] Everyone is at least being led by their dispositions.

Free will sceptic Saul Smilanksy expressed something along these lines when he told me that the issue is complicated, 'partly because it's philosophy and partly because philosophers are human beings and they come from different places and have different values. Even if there is agreement about different notions of free will, some philosophers will be – I think there's no other word – *temperamentally* inclined to set the bar high and therefore say that there is no free will, and others set the bar lower and say obviously there is free will, and some people like me will say it's complex and we have various bars. I'm even inclined to think that to some extent some people have an optimistic or pessimistic temperament, and therefore they tailor the bar that they intuitively feel will satisfy them.'

Smilansky is speculating about optimism and pessimism. But one study has come up with some empirical evidence that extraversion and introversion are correlated with beliefs about free will, concluding that 'extraversion predicts, to a significant extent, those who have compatibilist versus incompatibilist intuitions'.[16]

Many are appalled by this idea, as it goes against the whole notion that philosophy is about arguments, not arguers. But you only need to read the biographies and autobiographies of great philosophers to see that their personalities are intimately tied up with their ideas. W. V. O. Quine, for instance, recalled how as a toddler he sought the unfamiliar way home, which he interpreted as reflecting 'the thrill of discovery in theoretical science: the reduction of the unfamiliar to the familiar'.[17] Later, he was obsessed with crossing state lines and national borders, ticking each off on a list as he did so. Paul Feyerabend recalled how, not yet ten, he was enchanted by magic and mystery and wasn't affected by 'the many strange events that seemed to make up our world'.[18] Only a philosopher with delusions of her subject's objectivity would be surprised to find out that Quine and Feyerabend went on to write very different kinds of philosophy: Quine's in a formal, logical, systematising tradition (though typically on the limits of such formalisations); Feyerabend's anti-reductive and anti-systematising. It would take a great deal of faith in the objectivity of philosophy and philosophers to think that Feyerabend and Quine arrived at their respective philosophical positions simply by following the arguments where they led, when their inclinations so obviously seem to be in tune with their settled conclusions.[19]

Smilanksy is sanguine about what this means for philosophy, believing that the only way forward is for people to follow their own path. 'In a way it's like there used to be this notion of my station and my duties. You cannot be somebody else, you can try to understand people with different views, but in the end maybe the most productive thing is that you be obsessive and try to develop your position in the best way possible and then see what happens, whether it seems plausible to other people and what objections they have to it.'

There is more to this than just how personality affects the positions we adopt. It's also about what attitude we take to the position. Two people may agree exactly on the best way to describe the kind of freedom we have. But whereas one will take the attitude, 'that's good enough', that won't be good enough for others. I sometimes call this the problem of intonation. One person says, calmly, 'Human freedom consists in nothing more than the capacity to make choices and guide action in accordance with their settled, reflective beliefs and desires.' Another says the same thing, but an octave higher, with incredulity, the sentence ending with an alarmed exclamation mark, the 'nothing more' being a condemnation rather than a statement of fact.

What we see here is an emotional as well as a purely intellectual element in people's philosophical judgements. 'That's really an under-reflected-upon feature of philosophy, and I think there's a good reason for it,' says Dennett. 'It's dangerous, and even verges on the offensive to draw attention to the emotional stake that philosophers often have and betray in their argumentation. But that doesn't mean it's not there. I see it a lot. I see what I think is white-knuckled fear driving people to defend views that are not really well motivated, but they want to dig the moat a little further out than is defensible because they're afraid of the thin end of the wedge. I think that fear of the slippery slope motivates a lot of going for absolutes that just don't exist.' And it's because people have different temperaments and personalities that on an issue such as free will, where there are no killer facts to settle the debate, disagreements will continue until the end of time.

There is another dimension of subjective judgement that is also significant. You will have noticed that at several points in this book, there have been appeals to people's intuitions about free will. As Tamler Sommers observes, 'Philosophers working on free will and moral responsibility proceed almost exclusively by appealing to intuitions about principles and cases, and then developing theories to accommodate those intuitions.'[20]

The clearest definition of intuition in this context is the one Al Mele was taught as an undergraduate: 'A judgement or a belief, often about a case, that as far as possible doesn't derive from any theory you already hold. So you could think of it as gut reaction to a story.' No intuitions are pure. As Mele says, 'It turns out most of our judgements depend somewhat on tacit theories, so it's a matter of degree.' These intuitions need not be hardwired from birth or unchanging through life. They are simply the answers, solutions or explanations you find yourself feeling to be true, before you've thought through why they might be true.

Some say that many philosophical arguments lean too heavily on such intuitions. Mark Johnston, for example, has criticised reliance on what he calls the 'method of cases' in which 'Cases real and imaginary are produced. Competing accounts of the necessary and sufficient conditions ... are then evaluated simply in accord with how well they jibe with intuitions wrung from these cases.'[21] The worry is that despite all the careful argumentation and detailing of positions, at root the debate comes down to comparing intuitions.

Worse, it is not hard to find examples where what is in effect the same situation can elicit different intuitions depending on how it is presented. People are more inclined to support a policy that 'saves ten lives', for example, than one that 'fails to prevent ninety deaths', even if it is actually the precise same policy: an intervention that saves ten out of a hundred lives. As Johnston puts it, 'How can intuitions be reliable if we can be got to react so differently to the very same case?'[22]

And yet intuitions do appear to be the bedrock of many philosophical judgements. There was a wonderful piece of evidence for this at a conference I attended on free will. The speaker, a leading figure in the area, was being questioned by a member of the audience. Unconvinced by what the questioner was proposing, the speaker said, 'Is that what your theory tells you, or is it what you really think?' The question provoked laughter, but this was definitely the comedy of recognition. The joke depended on the listeners recognising that no matter how well they make a case, what they really think and believe to be true is determined by gut reaction. But if the view you hold intuitively is your real view, and anything else is second best, is all this intellectualising a bit of a game?

This is actually an instance of a much wider problem in philosophy, first articulated in Plato's *Meno*. In this dialogue, Socrates is trying to find the true meaning of virtue. Meno comes to believe that there is an element of paradox in looking for something that you do not yet know. As usual, it takes Socrates to articulate the problem clearly: 'A man cannot search either for what he knows or for what he does not know. He cannot search for what he knows – since he knows it, there is no need to search – nor for what he does not know, for he does not know what to look for.'[23]

The problem is very clear when applied to any enquiry to find a satisfactory definition of something, be it free will, virtue, knowledge or goodness. The way in which we do this is that someone will propose what appears to be a plausible definition. This will then be tested against examples where we think the concept ought to apply.

If the definition fits, it adds weight to the claim that it is a good one. If it doesn't, we need to revise it.

This sounds sensible, but the odd thing is that in order to know if the definition fits, in some sense you already have to know what the word means. But if you already know what the word means, why do you need a definition? Or why don't you already have a perfectly good one? The sense in which we 'already know' is clearly not that we have a worked-out theory or definition. Still, it seems this intuitive knowing is the ultimate criterion we have for judging whether a definition is correct or not (providing that it doesn't prove to be self-contradictory).

This problem is special to the kind of conceptual issues that philosophy deals with. It is not an issue in empirical matters such as science or history. For example, in physics, the question of whether dark matter exists is not one of definition. Dark matter is defined, and then experiments are conducted to see if it exists.

In theory, the problem of free will could be like this. We come up with one or more possible definitions of free will and then we see if there is evidence that we have it. In practice, though, the definitions are fundamental. Most people agree that free will, as defined by libertarians, does not exist, but as defined by compatibilists, it does. But that means the question of whether we have free will boils down to the question of which definition is right, and ultimately what decides that is not more evidence, but intuition.

This would all seem to be very unsatisfactory, and it certainly jars with the image of philosophy as pure rational inquiry, free from prejudice, hunch and personal judgement. But we need to acknowledge that intuition plays an ineliminable role in philosophical discussion. Can we make that concession without reducing philosophy to the mere exchanging of personal opinions?

I think we can. The reliance on intuitions is not as scandalous as it may seem. At the very least, as Randolph Clarke put it to me, 'It would seem rational to put a fair amount of weight on something that after careful consideration still seems to be true.' After all, it is not as though those things are impervious to new information and argument. Intuitions are not fixed from birth. By testing, probing and examining intuitions, and looking at what follows from maintaining them, we can in time change them. Many people, for example, when they first encounter the free will debate, have the very strong intuition that free will is not possible if all our thoughts and actions have to follow physical laws. But as they examine the issues more carefully and see that determinism does not entail bypassing, and that consciousness is an emergent property of physical systems (or as panpsychists claim, latent in all physical matter), their intuitions change.

There is therefore a two-way conversation between rational reflection and intuition, one informing the other. And as Saul Smilansky said to me, one thing that 'makes things seem more rational is if you can get sensible connections between things. So if your theories predict conclusions and then these conclusions happen to meet with your intuitions, then that lends support to both.'

But even if we think intuitions have a role to play, we might still ask: whose intuitions should count? Are some people more reliable witnesses? Does the process of having thought long and hard about an issue purify our intuitions or contaminate them? In recent years, there has been a growth in 'experimental philosophy', a major strand of which involves testing to see whether 'ordinary' people really have the intuitions that philosophers assume they have. Not everyone is enthusiastic about this. Timothy O'Connor says he is 'not that sanguine about the theoretical utility of asking ordinary folk, untainted by philosophical theorising, about how they feel about free will', in part because 'I'm sceptical about their ability to accurately report what they themselves actually think. It's difficult to tease out the principles of thinking that inform how you react to cases and exactly how you're thinking about certain concepts. I think ordinary people are often conflicted. That's part of the value of philosophy, to bring out conflicts in ordinary thought, to teach people to think very systematically and rigorously, and this is not something we're natively very good at.'

Eddy Nahmias, however, thinks there is a very good reason to consider the intuitions of people whose views have not been too infected by academic inquiry. If we ask why we are interested in the question of free will in the first place, it is because it appears to be 'associated with other things people care about, such as autonomy, self-development, creativity, morality, meaningful lives, and human relationships'. The most important meaning of 'free will' must therefore be one that actually relates to these lay concerns. If what we are interested in is part and parcel of ordinary life, then ordinary life, not scholastic definitions, must anchor our discussions. So, as Nahmias says, 'If debates about free will are not to focus on a technical concept, about which only the "expert" intuitions of trained philosophers are relevant,' then 'the relevant intuitions of non-philosophers' must matter.[24]

The vital point here is that, if intuitions do indeed matter, we should refer to more than just our own whenever possible. As Al Mele put it to me, 'We might too often think that most people think what we think, and that's something we should test.'

There is one more thing about free will that might explain why no one theory of it commands universal assent: it may not be a truly universal idea at all, but particular to modern western culture. Even within the West, we have already seen that the ancient Greeks lack the modern idea of free will, even though their ideas of responsibility appear to be very similar. There is some evidence, however, that there may be even more important differences around the world today about ideas of responsibility and freedom than there have been in the West over history.

The key area of difference appears to hinge on the relationship between free will and responsibility. Tamler Sommers argues that the western idea of responsibility rests on what he calls a 'robust control condition: in order to be genuinely blameworthy for a state of affairs, you must have played an active role in bringing it about'.[25] Indeed, the need for a control condition would seem to be obvious. How could you be held responsible for something you did not cause to happen?

However, 'like other intuitions and beliefs about moral responsibility', says Sommers, 'it is not nearly as universal as we might think'. He gives as an example the reaction by the Korean community in America to the shootings by Seung-Hui Cho at Virginia Tech in April 2007. Seung-Hui killed thirty-two people and injured seventeen others before committing suicide, in the worst massacre by a lone gunman in US history. The reaction of Hong Sung Pyo, a sixty-five-year-old textile executive in Seoul, was typical of many Koreans. 'We don't expect Koreans to shoot people, so we feel very ashamed and also worried.' It was this sense of shame that led the South Korean ambassador to the US to fast for thirty-two days, one for each of the murdered victims.[26]

Many Americans were baffled by this, but every expert on South Korea approached by a newspaper, television programme or magazine had the same explanation. 'It's a notion of collective responsibility,' said Mike Breen, author of *The Koreans*. 'I can smell a collective sense of guilt,' said Lim Jie-Hyun, a history professor at Hanyang University in Seoul. 'There is confusion [in Korea] between individual responsibility and national responsibility.' As Sommers concludes, 'Koreans did not merely feel shame for the act of the Virginia Tech killer, they felt responsible. They wished to apologise and atone for the act.'[27]

The psychologist Richard Nisbett has assembled an impressive array of evidence which suggests that deep cultural differences like these do actually change the way people think. In particular, the very idea of who performs an action differs across cultures. 'For Westerners,' writes Nisbett, 'it is the self that does the acting; for Easterners, action is something that is undertaken in concert with others or that is the consequence of the self operating in a field of forces.'[28] This means easterners have a sense of 'collective agency' largely absent in the West. Given that, it should not be surprising that there is not the same emphasis on a control condition in the East as in the West.

Korean culture is not the only one that does not require a control condition for responsibility. Sommers quotes the anthropologist Joseph Henrich, who says that it is 'common knowledge among anthropologists that in most small-scale societies you can be blamed for actions you don't intend to do'.[29] In several ancient myths, the control condition is even more conspicuously absent. Gods manipulate how people will act and then hold them responsible for what they do. Hence God tells Moses that when he visits the Pharoah, 'I will harden his heart so that he will not let the people go'. In Greek mythology, Agamemnon is compelled to murder his daughter, as Zeus sent Atë to confound his wits. But, says Sommers, 'In spite of the constraint *and* the manipulation, Clytemnestra and the chorus (in Aeschylus's version) hold Agamemnon morally responsible for the act.' This judgement 'is not illogical', but 'it is *counterintuitive* from a contemporary Western perspective'.[30]

Of course, it does not follow from this that notions of responsibility that do not have a control condition are no better or worse than those that do. Saul Smilansky responds to these kinds of cases with a robust defence of the superiority of modern, western ideas about personal responsibility. 'The fundamental idea that control is a condition for responsibility, and therefore for desert and just punishment, I think is a discovery,' he says, the roots of which can be found in the Bible in the rejection of the idea that 'you do not take the sins of the fathers upon the sons'. So 'if it is true that certain cultures do not respect this fundamental moral principle, then so much the worse for them; they just earn bad grades morally, from my side. The idea of punishing somebody who did not commit the crime, unless there is some very strange story going on, is a barbaric practice.'

Smilansky might well be right. However, I think it would be too quick to dismiss notions of responsibility that do not rest on a robust control condition as simply primitive, or misguided. A more positive way of looking at it is that responsibility is not some kind of morally basic notion, but one that is tied up with social practices. As such, it may be fitting that it appears in slightly different guises, depending on the social setting.

In the Korean example, to use a standard anthropological distinction, the key point is that, as is often the case in South and East Asia, Korea has a shame rather than a guilt culture. In shame cultures, the emphasis is on honour and maintaining face, usually collectively as a group. In guilt cultures, the emphasis is on the individual and on conscience. So, as Sommers puts it, 'if agents violate norms in a shame culture but the violation is undiscovered, the agents are less likely to hold themselves responsible; agents in guilt cultures will likely hold themselves responsible whether or not the offence is discovered'.[31]

To those who have grown up in a guilt culture, which is dominant (but not universal) in Christendom, shame cultures can appear bizarre. But it's not difficult to see how the guilt culture, taken to its logical conclusion, has absurdities of its own. Given what we know about the importance of nature and nurture, for example, isn't it actually unreasonable to hold the individual and the individual alone responsible for all the bad things they do? The control condition sounds sensible but no one can completely satisfy it, since we are simply not in control of everything that makes us who we are, and so of what we do.

Looked at in that light, what makes shame cultures different may not be that they lack the control condition, it might rather be that they attribute control to something wider than the individual. Koreans shared responsibility for Seung-Hui Cho's violence because they accepted that he was a product of their culture and not an atomised individual who acted in a vacuum.

Shame and guilt cultures may not be two alternative models, but rather ends of a spectrum. And it could be healthy not to be far out at either pole. You might remember ministerial responsibility, which I mentioned earlier, which is an example of people taking personal responsibility in a way that does not make sense on a highly individualistic guilt model. But perhaps that is precisely why it was a good convention. A healthy society needs to see responsibility falling at different levels, collectively and individually, and acting in whatever way is appropriate to the particular case.

Given all that we have considered in this chapter, it should not be surprising that philosophers, or indeed all those who philosophise, are not likely to end their disagreements about free will any time soon. That does not mean, however, that we cannot reach a kind of peace settlement in the dispute. All parties need to accept a few key things.

First, there is more than one notion of free will, and simply dismissing ones you disagree with as 'not really free will' won't do. Second, many of the ideas tied up with free will, such as responsibility, also admit of large variation, some of which is cultural. We do not need to hold that all are equally good in order to accept that we cannot just ignore or dismiss those we disagree with. Third, we have to be philosophically grown up and accept that there is an inevitable degree of imprecision and vagueness in many of the notions surrounding free will. 'Good enough' will sometimes have to be just that.

If we can accept all of this, then I think we can accept that there are legitimate notions of free will and responsibility that can help us to think about how we can take control of our own lives and what the limits on that control are. The last word on free will may not have been written, but we do know enough to come to the most important conclusions about it. It is to these that I shall now turn.

9

The Waiter

Many of the conversations I had for this book were conducted in restaurants and cafés. Each time this would remind me of the waiter described by Jean-Paul Sartre as an example of how we deny our freedom. Sartre's waiter so inhabits his role that he becomes a kind of robot, reducing himself to an object in the world rather than a subject with choice and agency.

'His movement is quick and forward, a little too precise, a little too rapid,' writes Sartre. 'He comes toward the patrons with a step a little too quick. He bends forward a little too eagerly; his voice, his eyes express an interest a little too solicitous for the order of the customer. Finally there he returns, trying to imitate in his walk the inflexible stiffness of some kind of automaton.'[1]

Sartre's waiter exemplifies the ways in which we convince ourselves that we have less choice than we do, believing ourselves to be prisoners of circumstance, our natures fixed. Imagining himself as this waiter, Sartre says that he would be acting 'as if it were not just in my power to confer their value and their urgency upon my duties and the right of my position, as if it were not my free choice to get up each morning at five o'clock or to remain in bed, even though it meant getting fired'. Sartre calls this denial of our own freedom 'bad faith'. We fall into it because we don't like the responsibility that comes with freedom. Every time we tell ourselves 'I have no choice', we are excused from taking responsibility for the consequences of our actions. It is not therefore difficult to imagine what Sartre would have had to say about the various denials of free will by neuro-scientists and sociologists. We want to say 'my brain made me do it', or 'it was my upbringing', because that absolves us from the respon-sibility.

For all its illustrative power, Sartre's example is somewhat unfair to waiters, who as far as I can tell are human beings with lives out-side of their work, trying to do a good job. The kind of waiter who stands in contrast to Sartre's is simply not a very good one. We all know what it is like to be served by someone who comes towards the patrons with a step a little too slow, who bends forward a little too reluctantly, his voice, his eyes expressing no interest in the order of the customer.

Sartre's example is also out of date. He explains that the waiter is playing a social role, and this requires that he give no hint that he has ideas above his station, just as 'a grocer who dreams is offen-sive to the buyer, because such a grocer is not wholly a grocer'. Nowadays, if anything, we assume the opposite: that of course a waiter is not wholly a waiter, and will be going off to travel the world or strum his guitar as soon as his shift is over. What is offensive to the customer is a waiter who makes it plain that he has no interest in waiting right now. Indeed, a waiter who comes across as wholly a waiter and nothing else would strike us as somewhat disturbing.

A more serious problem with Sartre's argument is that it over-states the extent to which we are free. Although we do indeed look to avoid responsibility too easily, it is not bad faith to accept that our choices are very much constrained by our biological, psychological and social pasts and presents. The usefulness of Sartre's ideas for me is that they suggest a direction of aspiration. Rather than looking to shrink the domain of our freedom by focusing on what is out of our control, we should look to extend it by coming to see how much we can actually control and change, accepting that the goal is not to control and change everything, since we can only be free within the limits of a real world not of our making.

Philosopher Ken Gemes put this well during a radio discussion of free will. He pointed out that Nietzsche, like Hume, thought that free actions were ones that flowed from character. However, unlike Hume, Nietzsche didn't believe everyone had character, 'a stable, unified and integrated hierarchy of drives'.[2] Character in this sense is only possessed by those who have achieved a harmony of first- and second-order desires, to use Harry Frankfurt's terminology. That makes free will 'a rare achievement rather than a natural endowment'.[3] This is not a new idea. Michael Frede identified something very similar in his examination of the idea of free will in antiquity. 'It is also crucial for the notion of the will that it is an ability which needs to be developed, cultivated, and perfected,' he wrote. 'One can get better and better at making choices, just as one can get worse and worse.'[4]

Gemes is right. What we are doing when we set out to think about free will is not merely to discover it, to find out if it is really there. It is to find out what we must do to make it real.

In order to become as free as we can be, we need to start by understanding what free will is. Unfortunately, we are starting in the midst of a thicket of misconceptions, one that has become thornier and more overgrown in recent years as philosophically naive scientists have dominated the debate. To get out, we need to cut away the most troublesome growths. This means rejecting ten myths of free will that have rooted themselves in the popular discourse. These myths and their corrections sum up the central arguments of the book.

*

Myth no. 1: *A choice cannot be free unless at the moment of choice you could have chosen other than you did.* It is not possible to make sense of this alleged capacity in a way that does not reduce choice to a random or capricious process. At the moment of any choice, the one you made was the only one you could have made. The feeling that you could have done otherwise is illusory. But this does not mean that it was not free. To say it was free is to say that it is a choice you made without coercion, on the basis of values and beliefs you endorse. It is also to say that you have the general capacities to make alternative choices at other times. The key concept is not 'could have done otherwise' but 'can in general do otherwise'.

Myth no. 2: *If your choices are predictable, they are not free.* Free choices can be entirely predictable. If you know someone well, you can know what they will freely choose. If you could see into the future, you would see what free people would choose. The capacity to alter the future unpredictably for no other reason than you can would be of no value.

Myth no. 3: *If a person could not have done other than as she did at the time of acting, she is not responsible for her actions.* Responsibility does not depend on having the ability to have done otherwise on any given occasion, but on generally being in control of our behaviour and having the ability to alter it. This kind of responsibility is not something we simply have or don't have. It is something we place on others and something we take on ourselves. To become free is to embrace responsibility, not to shirk from it.

Myth no. 4: *If a choice is free, you must be conscious that you have made it.* Many of our choices are made automatically or unconsciously, yet they are still free. We can see this most clearly in the case of artists, who often have no idea where their ideas come from. Yet these creative 'choices' are archetypes of freedom, not counter-examples to it.

Myth no. 5: *If a choice is free, you must know why you have made it.* Even our free choices can be in some sense mysterious to those who make them. Being free does not require that we are completely transparent to ourselves.

Myth no. 6: *Freedom of thought requires that you have chosen your own beliefs.* No belief worth having is the product of pure, unconditioned choice. What makes thought free is that it is sufficiently informed and not coerced. To freely believe what is evidently true is to submit to the necessity of reason, not to exercise some independent faculty of willing.

Myth no. 7: *Neuroscience threatens to prove – or may have proved already – that free will is an illusion.* Science can only make clearer why a particular common misconception of free will as an escape from the causal necessity of the physical world is false. But we don't even need science to prove that, since the very idea is incoherent. All free will requires from science is confirmation that human beings are self-organising, self-regulating organisms whose conscious beliefs, desires and deliberations affect their actions. Nothing in science has challenged this and much has supported it.

Myth no. 8: *Everything not under our control diminishes our freedom.* On the contrary, much of what we most value about our freedom depends on things we cannot change: freedom to love another, to believe $2 + 2 = 4$, to pursue values we cannot help but endorse.

Myth no. 9: *Free will is a single capacity.* Freedom can involve more or less spontaneity, originality, conscious deliberation and independence from the control of others. Some find ways of expressing their free will fulsomely in conditions of very little political freedom. Some exercise their freedom with little originality or creativity; others are extremely creative without being particularly intellectually reflective. These people all express freedom in different forms.

Myth no. 10: *People either have free will or they don't.* Freedom is a matter of a degree. It is a capacity we can have more or less of; enhance or diminish. A well-developed free will is not a universal gift from birth but an achievement we need to strive for.

The moral philosopher Susan Wolf makes a very important observation, which applies to the idea of free will I am endorsing. 'The condition of freedom cannot be stated in terms that are value-free,' she says. 'Thus, the problem of free will has been misrepresented insofar as it has been thought to be a purely metaphysical problem.'[5] If a proper account of free will is not merely a description, but a prescription for who we aspire to be, then it is an issue of politics and ethics, not just science and metaphysics.

When we think about the promotion of human freedom as a political goal, we tend to think of the limited objective of removing the shackles of state tyranny. But of course, social reformers of the past have also seen the importance of education, health care and social security as enablers of a more positive kind of freedom. There are, however, tensions in the twin desiderata of an enabling state and an unconstrained citizenry. A mature politics has to accept that there is value in both, rather than justifying all state meddling as a means to help people fulfil their potential, or decrying all such initiatives as unacceptable infringements of personal liberty.

This balancing act is usually seen in terms of trade-offs between positive and negative freedom: freedom from coercion and freedom to flourish. However, instead of seeing this problem as being one of reconciling two different notions of political freedom, I propose that we think instead of a single, more coherent notion of human freedom and how our politics can serve its flourishing.

Here's what I have in mind. To be free, I have argued, is to maximise the kind of autonomy and responsibility we really can have while fully accepting the things over which we have no control. The state's primary role is to enable us to maximise this freedom. Not the shallow freedom to choose between a hundred breakfast cereals, but the capacity for autonomy and self-regulation. This means, wherever possible, treating people as autonomous, responsible citizens and not as subjects who need looking after.

Of course, it is not always easy to know in any given context how able people are to govern themselves. Would it not be cruel to leave some people with learning disabilities largely unsupervised, to 'respect their autonomy'? Don't some people who are mentally ill need to be sectioned – taken into psychiatric care against their will? These are hard questions, and I do not pretend to know enough about either of these kinds of cases to reach a judgement. But I think that when we need to decide on which side we should err, it should be on the side of freedom. The risks of overstating the extent to which we are not in control are high. Historically, we have seen too many cases of people being locked away or medicated against their will, supposedly for their own good.

The ability to self-regulate is undermined by the belief that we cannot. Responsibility is not taken unless it is placed upon us. Therefore the state should be very careful about basing its practices on any assumptions that we are less able to govern our own behaviour than we think. Education and the criminal justice system must not make too much of the fact that people are the products of their genes and upbringings. Of course, these factors must be taken into consideration. But we need to get over the crude distinction between criminals as entirely responsible or mere victims of genes, upbringing and environment. Punishment needs to retain a sense of holding people to account if it is to enable criminals to develop their freedom, just as it must involve the kind of rehabilitation that builds their sense of agency.

Some libertarians like to stop there, emphasising only the extent to which the state needs to butt out. But that would be to ignore the extent to which our freedom is extremely limited. I think the state has a role trying to iron out some of the injustices that result from things over which people have no control or responsibility. It is not by our free will that we are born into rich or poor families, have high or low IQ, suffer from disabilities or inherit debilitating medical conditions. Nature does not dispense her gifts according to any principles of justice. The great achievement of human civilisation is the development of ethics and morality, which see that the way things are is not necessarily the way they ought best to be, and that what is natural is not always good. So where there are inequalities purely by accident of birth, it is a moral achievement to say that we will not simply accept them, but use the apparatus of the state to try to mitigate them.

Furthermore, the state's job is to coordinate the kinds of actions we can only achieve, or achieve better, cooperatively. Transport infrastructure is the obvious example, but so also are education and health care. We always have to question whether the state is a better provider than business of such collective goods, but there is no obvious reason to think government is bound to infringe our liberty more than business. State bodies are accountable to the entire electorate, while companies are only accountable to consumers with the option to take their money elsewhere.

More contentiously, I see no reason why we cannot freely choose to limit what we are legally free to do. Just as Homer's Ulysses freely chose to tie himself to the mast so he did not have to rely on willpower alone to resist the Sirens, we can freely choose to limit the sale or advertising of certain goods to remove from the public domain sources of temptation we don't want. Regulation can also be a way of dealing with the limits on our time. *Caveat emptor* – buyer beware – is in theory a fine principle of individual autonomy, but I'd much rather give up some of that in favour of sensible health and safety legislation so I don't always have to worry about whether my doctor is competent or whether my new heater is likely to burst into flames.

In short, we can see that the state's role is not to balance positive and negative freedoms, but to help mitigate social problems that are beyond the control of individual free choice and to coordinate the free choices of the citizenry. It ought to do both things in such ways that maximise citizens' capacities to live as responsible, autonomous agents.

This proposal is significantly different to the currently fashionable idea that government ought to promote Gross Domestic Happiness rather than Gross Domestic Product, well-being rather than national wealth. I don't actually think that the idea that GDP is the be-all and end-all of government has ever had many sincere supporters. The alternative may look attractive, but it contains within it a dangerous threat to autonomy, namely, that you can only pursue this policy if you have an idea of what human well-being comprises. Such ideas have a habit of being extremely value-laden. Promoting well-being sounds unobjectionable until you discover that it might mean promoting marriage, religious belief or being happy with what you have rather than struggling to change society.

The alternative is not value-free but it is value-minimal. The best articulation of it is the capabilities approach developed by Amartya Sen and Martha Nussbaum. This argues that the relative development of countries should be assessed on the basis of the extent to which they enable citizens to develop their capabilities in the ways they choose. This means measuring not just GDP – although that is important since the richer a country the more, on average, its citizens can do – but also assessing factors such as health, gender equality, freedom of association and religion. The focus is on what provides a strong social basis for people to freely pursue their own visions of the good life, not trying to build society on the basis of one such vision.[6]

A sense that we are capable of making choices for ourselves and shaping our own futures appears to be universal and central to how we think of ourselves and others. This feeling is neither a complete illusion nor quite as it appears to be. Freedom can be saved from the clutches of neuroscientists and determinists, but it has to be changed in the process.

First and foremost, we have to jettison the libertarian idea that we can make choices that are completely undetermined by the past. That's good news, because it is hard to see how such a capacity could exist and why it would be worth having if it did. What's more, the claim that a belief in libertarian free will is essential for moral, purposive action just doesn't seem to stand up. As Tamler Sommers observes, 'There is no evidence whatsoever that a belief in libertarian free will and moral responsibility played even the slightest role in motivating people like King, Gandhi, and other less celebrated heroes who risked their lives to help others.'[7]

Modern writers on free will have often borrowed Borges's image of the garden of forking paths to illustrate what free will means. In this metaphor, the future always contains more than one possible route, and to be free is to decide for ourselves which one to follow. John Martin Fischer asks what would happen if this 'natural and intuitive view' proved to be false, and argues that it might not matter as much as we think. 'In this case, what matters is how we proceed – how we walk down that path,' he writes. 'When we walk down the path of life with courage, or resilience, or compassion, we might not (for all we know) make a certain sort of difference, but we do make a distinctive kind of statement.'[8] What matters most in life is what we do and how we do it, not that we might have done otherwise.

A realistic view of free will does require a greater sense of how much is not of our choosing. But this need not lead us to any kind of despair. Sam Harris, who I think is wrong to deny free will, nonetheless shows how a modest acceptance of freedom's limits can make us better people. 'Losing the sense of free will has only improved my ethics,' he writes, 'by increasing my feelings of compassion and forgiveness, and diminishing my sense of entitlement to the fruits of my own good luck.'[9]

Experience bears this out. The less we understand about why people do what they do and attribute it to nothing more than whim, the more likely we are to judge them harshly. Greater understanding almost always leads to better, more truthful judgements. Think about the people closest to you. Over time you become more aware of the things the people you love can't change about themselves, and you may even understand why. The result of that is not that you love or care for them less. You take their limitations on board and your love deepens.

The idea that we don't need the particular modern, western conception of free will in order to believe that we still have something worthy of the name is strongly supported by Michael Frede's analysis of the idea of free will in antiquity, where he finds it almost entirely absent. The alternative idea of freedom that stands in its place, though flawed in detail, he finds 'rather attractive'. It centres on the idea that to live a good life means being able to make the right choices, and that we are prevented from making such choices by 'false beliefs or irrational attachments and aversions'. To be free is to liberate ourselves from these things, which we can do because 'the world does not systematically force these beliefs, attachments and aversions on us'.

The realistic view of free will that I commend understands the notion of freedom at the appropriate human scale. It steers a course between the hubris of believing we are unconditioned, completely free agents, and the fatalism of believing we are mere puppets of the laws of nature. It encourages us to be compassionate towards others, accepting that they are not entirely responsible for who they are, but also to hold them to account and so encourage them to grasp as much control over their own destinies as they can. And it also allows us to accept that much is not of our choosing, because that is the only way we could be capable of making any choices at all. There are myths and illusions surrounding free will, but free will itself is far from illusory. It is as real as we find ourselves ready to make it.

Acknowledgements

Many thanks to my editor Bella Lacey for her careful and skilful comments on the first draft, and to her predecessor Sara Holloway and my agent Lizzy Kremer for getting the project off the ground. Thanks also to Jenny Page, whose keen eye helped weed out the clunky and inelegant. The whole Granta team – Iain Chapple, Sara D'Arcy, Christine Lo, Colin Midson, Aidan O'Neill, Angela Rose, Sarah Wasley – have been supportive throughout.

Thanks also to all the people who agreed to be interviewed for the book: Gwen Adshead, Andrei Aliaksandrau, Patricia Churchland, Randolph Clarke, Eileen Craven, Daniel C. Dennett, David Eagleman, Ismail Einashe, 'Fergus', Harry Frankfurt, Margaret Hooper, Ann Jeremiah, Ma Jian, Al Mele, Shaun Nichols, Timothy O'Connor, Grayson Perry, 'Peter', Edward Rees, Rahela Sidiqi, Saul Smilansky, Tim Spector and Judy Tabbott. Rachael Jolley from Index on Censorship helped set up the discussion with the dissidents, while Victoria Vazquez at the Department of Twin Research, King's College London was enormously helpful in introducing me to identical twins. My apologies to all others who helped but whose contributions I have forgotten.

Finally, thanks to my better half Antonia for her tireless support and encouragement, as well as innumerable enlightening conversations about the issues in this book.

Notes

Introduction

1 Nora Barlow (ed.), *The Autobiography of Charles Darwin 1809–1882* (Collins, 1958), p. 87
2 1929 interview reported in Ronald W. Clark, *Einstein: The Life and Times* (HarperCollins, 1984), p. 422
3 Albert Einstein, *The World as I See It* (Filiquarian Publishing, 2006), p. 12
4 Stephen Hawking, *Black Holes and Baby Universes and Other Essays* (Bantam, 1994), p. 116
5 Richard Dawkins, *The Selfish Gene* (Oxford University Press, 1976), p. v
6 Sam Harris, *Free Will* (Free Press, 2012), p. 6
7 Interview in *Mail On Sunday*, 21 February 1993
8 Clare Tickell, 'The Early Years: Foundations for life, health and learning: An Independent Report on the Early Years Foundation Stage to Her Majesty's Government' (Department for Education, 2011) p. 8 www.gov.uk/government/uploads/system/uploads/attachment_data/file/180919/DFE-00177-2011.pdf
9 'Behavioural Insight Team Paper on Fraud, Error and Debt' (Cabinet Office, 2012), p. 16 www.gov.uk/government/publications/fraud-error-and-debt-behavioural-insights-team-paper

PART ONE: FREEDOM UNDER THREAT

Chapter 1: The Demon

1 Pierre-Simon Laplace, 'A Philosophical Essay on Probabilities' (1814)
2 Augustine, 'On Free Choice of the Will' in Derk Pereboom (ed.), *Free Will* (Hackett, 2009), p. 32
3 Peter van Inwagen, *An Essay on Free Will* (Clarendon Press, 1983), pp. 16, 56
4 Ray Bradbury, 'A Sound of Thunder' in *R is for Rocket* (Doubleday, 1952)
5 John Martin Fischer, Robert Kane, Derk Pereboom and Manuel Vargas, *Four Views on Free Will* (Blackwell, 2007), p. 208
6 T. H. Huxley, 'On the Hypothesis that Animals are Automata, and its History', *The Fortnightly Review*, 16 (New series, 1874), pp. 555–80
7 John Searle, *Minds, Brains and Science* (Penguin, 1984), p. 17
8 Lucretius, *De rerum natura*, trans. William Ellery Leonard (Internet Classics Archive) http://classics.mit.edu/Carus/nature_things.html
9 Jean Meslier, *Superstition In All Ages* (1732), trans. Anna Knoop (1878), §LXXX (Project Gutenberg) www.gutenberg.org/ebooks/17607
10 Paul Henri Thiery (Baron D'Holbach), *The System of Nature*, vol. 1 (1770) (Project Gutenberg) www.gutenberg.org/ebooks/8909
11 Nick Spencer, *Atheists: The Origin of the Species* (Bloomsbury, 2014), p. 112
12 Henry Drummond, *The Lowell Lectures on the Ascent of Man* (Phoenix University of Theology Digital Library) http://put.phxut.us/library/index.htm
13 See chapter four, 'Soul searching' in my book *The Ego Trick* (Granta, 2011), pp. 60–72
14 Michael Frede, *A Free Will* (University of California Press, 2011), p. 10
15 Friedrich Beck and John C. Eccles, 'Quantum aspects of brain activity and the role of consciousness', *Proceedings of the National*

Notes

Academy of Sciences of the United States of America, 89 (23) (1992), pp. 11357–61

16 Robert Kane, *Free Will* (Blackwell, 2002), p. 284
17 Tamler Sommers, *Relative Justice* (Princeton University Press, 2012), p. 92
18 John Martin Fischer, Robert Kane, Derk Pereboom and Manuel Vargas, *Four Views on Free Will* (Blackwell, 2007), p. 26
19 Ibid., p. 29
20 Immanuel Kant, *Critique of Pure Reason*, in Derk Pereboom (ed.), *Free Will* (Hackett, 2009), p. 107
21 Robert Kane, *Free Will* (Blackwell, 2002), pp. 24–5
22 Immanuel Kant, *Critique of Pure Reason* in Derk Pereboom (ed.), *Free Will* (Hackett, 2009), pp.105–6
23 Ibid., p. 116
24 Arthur Schopenhauer, *The Two Fundamental Problems of Ethics* [1840], trans. David E. Cartwright and Edward E. Erdmann (Oxford University Press, 2010)
25 M. R. Bennett and P. M. S. Hacker, *Foundations of Neuroscience* (Wiley-Blackwell, 2003), p. 68ff
26 Gary Younge, 'He shoots. He scores. He folds his socks', *Guardian* (*G2* section), 18 May 2006, p. 18

PART TWO: FREEDOM LOST

Chapter 2: The Neuroscientist

1 For the Libet experiments see Benjamin Libet, Curtis A. Gleason, Elwood W. Wright and Dennis K. Pearl, 'Time of Conscious Intention to Act in Relation to Onset of Cerebral Activity (Readiness-Potential) – The Unconscious Initiation of a Freely Voluntary Act', *Brain*, 106 (1983), pp. 623–42; and Benjamin Libet, 'Unconscious Cerebral Initiative and the Role of Conscious Will in Voluntary Action', *The Behavioral and Brain Sciences*, 8 (1985), pp. 529–66
2 Sam Harris, *Free Will* (Free Press, 2012), p. 8

3 Caroline Williams, 'Brain imaging spots our abstract choices before we do', *New Scientist*, 10 April 2013

4 *In Our Time*, BBC Radio Four, 10 March 2011

5 J. A. Bargh, M. Chen and L. Burrows, 'Automaticity of social behavior: Direct effects of trait construct and stereotype activation on action', *Journal of Personality and Social Psychology*, 71 (1996), pp. 230–44

6 Kathleen D. Vohs and Jonathan W. Schooler, 'The Value of Believing in Free Will: Encouraging a Belief in Determinism Increases Cheating', *Psychological Science*, vol. 19, no. 1 (2008), pp. 49–54

7 Dick Swaab, *We Are Our Brains* (Allen Lane, 2014), p. 4

8 Galen Strawson, 'Real Naturalism', *London Review of Books*, vol. 35, no. 18, 26 September 2013, pp. 28–30

9 Ibid.

10 J. B. S. Haldane, *Possible Worlds and Other Papers* [1927] (Transaction Publishers, 2002), p. 286

11 Colin McGinn, *The Mysterious Flame: Conscious Minds in a Material World* (Basic Books, 1999), pp. 97–9

12 Philip W. Anderson, 'More is Different', *Science*, 177 (4047) (1972), pp. 393–6

13 Robert Laughlin, *A Different Universe* (Basic Books, 2006), p. 76

14 Grégoire Nicolis and Catherine Rouvas-Nicolis, 'Complex systems', *Scholarpedia*, 2 (11): 1473 (2007), www.scholarpedia.org/article/Complex_systems

15 Michael Gazzaniga, *Who's in Charge?* (Ecco, 2011), p. 124

16 Ibid., p. 127

17 Ibid., p. 107

18 J. M. Burns and R. H. Swerdlow, 'Right orbitofrontal tumor with pedophilia symptom and constructional apraxia sign', *Archives of Neurology*, 60 (3), 172 (2003), pp. 437–40

19 Michael Gazzaniga, *Who's in Charge?* (Ecco, 2011), pp. 68, 103

20 Video at www.thebrainandthemind.co.uk/The_Talks/Talk1/

21 Ewen Callaway, 'Brain scanner predicts your future moves', *New Scientist*, 13 April 2008

22 E. M. Forster, *Aspects of the Novel* [1927] (Penguin, 1990), p. 99

23 Benedict Spinoza, *Ethics* in Derk Pereboom (ed.), *Free Will* (Hackett, 2009), p. 63

Notes

David Hume, *An Enquiry Concerning Human Understanding* in Derk Pereboom (ed.), *Free Will* (Hackett, 2009), p. 96
25 Sam Harris, *Free Will* (Free Press, 2012), p. 64
26 Ibid., p. 13
27 Aristotle, *Nicomachean Ethics* in Derk Pereboom (ed.), *Free Will* (Hackett, 2009), p. 4
28 Saul Smilansky, 'Fischer's Way: The Next Level', *The Journal of Ethics*, vol. 12, no. 2 (2008), pp. 147–55
29 P. F. Strawson, 'Freedom and Resentment' in Derk Pereboom (ed.), *Free Will* (Hackett, 2009), p. 164
30 Sam Harris, *Free Will* (Free Press, 2012), p. 340
31 Eddy Nahmias, 'Intuitions about Free Will, Determinism and Bypassing' in Robert Kane (ed.), *The Oxford Handbook of Free Will* (Oxford University Press, 2011), pp. 560–61
32 Ibid., p. 567

Chapter 3: The Geneticist

1 Tim Spector, *Identically Different* (Phoenix, 2012), pp. 7–8
2 Daniel E. Koshland, 'Sequences and Consequences of the Human Genome', *Science*, 246 (1989), p. 189
3 ABC News, 26 June 2000, archived at http://abcnews.go.com/Archives/video/human-genome-map-dna-10190454
4 Nigel Eastman and Colin Campbell, 'Neuroscience and legal determination of criminal responsibility', *Nature Reviews Neuroscience*, 7, pp. 311–18 (April 2006)
5 Steve Jones, *The Language of the Genes* (HarperCollins, 1993), p. 180
6 Bertrand Russell, *Why I Am Not a Christian* (George Allen & Unwin, 1957), p. 9
7 E. M. Forster, 'What I Believe', *The Nation*, 16 July 1938
8 Galen Strawson, 'The Impossibility of Ultimate Moral Responsibility' in Derk Pereboom (ed.), *Free Will* (Hackett, 2009), p. 299
9 Friedrich Nietzsche, *Beyond Good and Evil* [1886], trans. R. J. Hollingdale (Penguin, 1973), p. 32 (§8)
10 John Martin Fischer, Robert Kane, Derk Pereboom and Manuel Vargas, *Four Views on Free Will* (Blackwell, 2007), p. 14

11 Ibid., p. 67

12 Saul Smilansky, 'Free Will, Fundamental Dualism, and the Centrality of Illusion' in Robert Kane (ed.), *The Oxford Handbook of Free Will* (Oxford University Press, 2011), p. 428

13 Dick Swaab, *We Are Our Brains* (Allen Lane, 2014), pp. 326–30

14 Michael Frede, *A Free Will* (University of California Press, 2011), p. 4

15 Ibid., p. 15

16 Tatian, *Oratio ad Graecos*, trans. J. E. Reynolds in Philip Shaff (ed.), *Ante-Nicene Fathers*, vol. 2, p. 128 www.ccel.org/ccel/schaff/anf02.html

17 Augustine, *On Free Choice of the Will* in Derk Pereboom (ed.), *Free Will* (Hackett, 2009), p. 20

18 Michael Frede, *A Free Will* (University of California Press, 2011), p. 161

19 Martin Luther, *The Bondage of The Will* [1525], trans. Philip S. Watson, www.lutheransonline.com/lo/671/FSLO-1344356671-111671.pdf

20 Erasmus, 'A Discussion or Discourse concerning Free Will' [1524] in *Erasmus and Luther: The Battle over Free Will*, ed. Clarence H. Miller (Hackett, 2012), p. 29

21 Michael Frede, *A Free Will* (University of California Press, 2011), pp. 103–5

PART THREE: FREEDOM REGAINED

Chapter 4: The Artist

1 Diana Athill, 'Falling short: seven writers reflect on failure', *Guardian* (*Review* section), 22 June 2013, p. 2

2 Allegra Donn, 'Vangelis: why *Chariots of Fire*'s message is still important today', *Observer*, 1 July 2012, p. 24

3 Ray Bradbury, *Zen in the Art of Writing* (Joshua Odell Editions, 1994), p. 116

4 Anne Lamott, *Bird by Bird* (Anchor Books, 1980), p. 182

Notes

5 Ernest Hemingway, *By-Line Ernest Hemingway: Selected Articles and Dispatches of Four Decades*, ed. William White (Scribner, 1998), p. 217

6 *Life Lessons* is one of three short films in *New York Stories* (Woody Allen, Francis Ford Coppola, Martin Scorsese, USA, 1989)

7 'Living with Autism', video on Seth's website http://growyourbrainart.com/biography/press/

8 Jacky Klein, *Grayson Perry* (Thames & Hudson, 2013), p. 190

9 Michael Gazzaniga, *Who's in Charge?* (Ecco, 2011), p. 44

10 Julian Baggini, *The Ego Trick* (Granta, 2011)

11 Douglas R. Hofstadter and Daniel C. Dennett, *The Mind's I* (Bantam Books, 1982), p. 191

Chapter 5: The Dissident

1 Ted Honderich (ed.), *The Oxford Companion to Philosophy* (Oxford University Press, 2005), p. 312

2 Michael Frede, *A Free Will* (University of California Press, 2011), p. 9

3 Isaiah Berlin, 'Two Concepts of Liberty' [1958] in Isaiah Berlin, *Liberty* (Oxford University Press, 2002)

4 Jean-Paul Sartre, 'The Republic of Silence' in A. J. Liebling (ed.), *Republic of Silence* (Harcourt, Brace & Co., 1947), pp. 498–500

5 'Oprah Talks to Paul Rusesabagina', *O, The Oprah Magazine*, March 2006

6 Susan Wolf, 'Asymmetrical Freedom' in Derk Pereboom (ed.), *Free Will* (Hackett, 2009), p. 232

7 Ibid., pp. 229–30

8 Michael Frede, *A Free Will* (University of California Press, 2011), p. 29

9 Ibid., p. 101

10 This quote is widely attributed to Buridan but I cannot locate the original source.

11 René Descartes, *Meditations on First Philosophy*, §432–3 in *Descartes: Selected Writings*, trans. John Cottingham, Robert Stoothoff, Dugald Murdoch (Cambridge University Press, 1998), pp. 134–5. Thanks to Randolph Clarke for the pointer.

225

PART FOUR: FREEDOM DIMINISHED

Chapter 6: The Psychopath

1 Daniel C. Dennett, *Intuition Pumps and Other Tools for Thinking* (Allen Lane, 2013), p. 408
2 Sam Harris, *Free Will* (Free Press, 2012), p. 17
3 Ibid., p. 4
4 Ibid., p. 53
5 Richard Dawkins, 'Let's all stop beating Basil's car', *Edge*, 2006, www.edge.org/q2006/q06_9.html
6 P. F. Strawson, 'Freedom and Resentment' in Derk Pereboom (ed.), *Free Will* (Hackett, 2009), p. 151
7 Tamler Sommers, *Relative Justice* (Princeton University Press, 2012), p. 170
8 Dick Swaab, *We Are Our Brains* (Allen Lane, 2014), p. 396
9 Gwen Adshead, 'Vice and Viciousness', *Philosophy, Psychiatry, & Psychology*, vol. 15, no. 1 (2008), pp. 23–6
10 'Daniel M'Naghten's Case', United Kingdom House of Lords Decisions, 26 May, 19 June 1843
11 Sam Harris, *Free Will* (Free Press, 2012), p. 52
12 Daniel Dennett, *The Intentional Stance* (MIT Press, 1987), p. 17
13 P. F. Strawson, 'Freedom and Resentment' in Derk Pereboom (ed.), *Free Will* (Hackett, 2009), p. 161
14 Sam Harris, *Free Will* (Free Press, 2012), p. 49
15 Michael Frede, *A Free Will* (University of California Press, 2011), pp. 25–6
16 John Martin Fischer, Robert Kane, Derk Pereboom and Manuel Vargas, *Four Views on Free Will* (Blackwell, 2007), p. 115
17 David Hume, *A Treatise of Human Nature* [1738], Part III, §II in Derk Pereboom (ed.), *Free Will* (Hackett, 2009), p. 85
18 Michael Frede, *A Free Will* (University of California Press, 2011), p. 11
19 Patricia Churchland, *Braintrust* (Princeton University Press, 2011), p. 9

20 Julian Baggini, 'Interview with Patricia Churchland', *The Philosophers' Magazine*, issue 57, 2nd quarter 2012, p. 63

21 Tamler Sommers, *Relative Justice* (Princeton University Press, 2012), p. 36

22 Michael Gazzaniga. *Who's in Charge?* (Ecco, 2011), p. 108

23 Ibid., p. 137

24 Joshua Knobe, 'Intentional Action in Folk Psychology: An Experimental Investigation', *Philosophical Psychology*, 16 (2003), pp. 309–24

25 Daniel M. Wegner, *The Illusion of Conscious Will* (Bradford Books, 2002), p. 342

26 Saul Smilansky, 'Free Will, Fundamental Dualism, and the Centrality of Illusion', in Robert Kane (ed.), *The Oxford Handbook of Free Will* (Oxford University Press, 2011), pp. 440, 434

27 Sam Harris, *Free Will* (Free Press, 2012), p. 47

28 Michael Frede, *A Free Will* (University of California Press, 2011), pp. 76, 67

29 David Hume, *An Enquiry Concerning Human Understanding* [1748], §8 in Derk Pereboom (ed.), *Free Will* (Hackett, 2009), p. 98

30 John Martin Fischer, Robert Kane, Derk Pereboom and Manuel Vargas, *Four Views on Free Will* (Blackwell, 2007), p. 160

31 Ibid., p. 78

32 Ibid., p. 79

33 Roy F. Baumeister, E. J. Masicampo and C. Nathan DeWall, 'Prosocial Benefits of Feeling Free: Disbelief in Free Will Increases Aggression and Reduces Helpfulness', *Personality and Social Psychology Bulletin*, vol. 35, no. 2, February 2009, pp. 260–68

34 Hanna Pickard, 'Responsibility without blame: philosophical reflections on clinical practice' in K. W. M. Fulford, M. Davies, R. T. Gipps, G. Graham, J. Sadler, G. Strangellini and T. Thornton (eds), *The Oxford Handbook of Philosophy of Psychiatry* (Oxford University Press, 2013), pp. 1134–50

35 Adrian Raine, *The Anatomy of Violence* (Allen Lane, 2013), pp. 335–6

36 Ibid., pp. 68, 104

37 Ibid., p. 339

38 Ibid., p. 47

39 Ibid., pp. 283–8
40 Sentencing Guidelines Council, *Magistrates' Court Sentencing Guidelines* (2008), p. 16
41 Reoffending rates are published regularly at www.gov.uk. Figure quoted is from latest available statistics at time of writing at www.gov.uk/government/publications/proven-reoffending-statistics-april-2011-march-2012
42 John Martin Fischer, Robert Kane, Derk Pereboom and Manuel Vargas, *Four Views on Free Will* (Blackwell, 2007), p. 115
43 Sam Harris, *Free Will* (Free Press, 2012), p. 58
44 John Martin Fischer, Robert Kane, Derk Pereboom and Manuel Vargas, *Four Views on Free Will* (Blackwell, 2007), p. 155

Chapter 7: The Addict

1 Hanna Pickard, 'Responsibility without blame: philosophical reflections on clinical practice' in K. W. M. Fulford, M. Davies, R. T. Gipps, G. Graham, J. Sadler, G. Strangellini and T. Thornton (eds), *The Oxford Handbook of Philosophy of Psychiatry* (Oxford University Press, 2013), p. 1138
2 Alcoholics Anonymous, *The Big Book* (4th edn) www.aa.org/pages/en_US/alcoholics-anonymous, p. 59
3 Roy F. Baumeister and John Tierney, *Willpower: Rediscovering our Greatest Strength* (Allen Lane, 2012), p. 5
4 Ibid., pp. 36–7
5 Arthur Schopenhauer, 'On the Freedom of the Will' [1839] in *The Two Fundamental Problems of Ethics*, trans. David E. Cartwright and Edward E. Erdmann (Oxford University Press, 2010), p. 44
6 Gilbert Ryle, *The Concept of Mind* (Penguin, 1963), pp. 61–80
7 K. C. Berridge and T. E. Robinson, 'What is the role of dopamine in reward: hedonic impact, reward learning, or incentive salience?', *Brain Research Reviews*, 28 (3), December 1998, pp. 309–69.
8 For more on Toates's work in this area, see *How Sexual Desire Works* (Cambridge University Press, 2014)

9　Harry Frankfurt, 'Freedom of the will and the concept of a person' in *The Importance of What We Care About* (Cambridge University Press, 1998), p. 21

10　Benedict Spinoza, *Ethics* [1677], Part I, prop. 33 (Hackett, 1982), p. 54

11　Ibid., Part I, def. 7, p. 31

12　John Martin Fischer, Robert Kane, Derk Pereboom and Manuel Vargas, *Four Views on Free Will* (Blackwell, 2007), p. 189

PART FIVE: FREEDOM EARNED

Chapter 8: The Philosopher

1　P. F. Strawson, 'Freedom and Resentment' in Derk Pereboom (ed.), *Free Will* (Hackett, 2009), p. 149

2　Nicholas Rescher, *Philosophical Reasoning* (Wiley-Blackwell, 2001), p. 93

3　David Hume, *An Enquiry Concerning Human Understanding* [1748], §8 in Derk Pereboom (ed.), *Free Will* (Hackett, 2009), p. 87

4　Tamler Sommers, *Relative Justice* (Princeton, University Press, 2012), p. 72

5　See, for example, E. H. Rosch (1973), 'Natural categories', *Cognitive Psychology*, 4 (3), pp. 328–50

6　Harry Frankfurt, 'On Bullshit' in *The Importance of What We Care About* (Cambridge University Press, 1998), p. 117

7　Julian Baggini, 'Stirring Shit', *The Philosophers' Magazine*, 31 (2005), p. 88

8　John Martin Fischer, Robert Kane, Derk Pereboom and Manuel Vargas, *Four Views on Free Will* (Blackwell, 2007), p. 180

9　Sam Harris, *Free Will* (Free Press, 2012), p. 20

10　All quoted in John Martin Fischer, Robert Kane, Derk Pereboom and Manuel Vargas, *Four Views on Free Will* (Blackwell, 2007), p. 45

11　Ibid., p. 209

12 Ibid., pp. 146–7
13 Ibid., pp. 215, 163, 210
14 Lee Siegel, *Net of Magic: Wonders and Deceptions in India* (University of Chicago Press, 1991), p. 425
15 Plato, *The Republic* 394d (Penguin, 1974), p. 152
16 Adam Feltz and Edward T. Cokely, 'Do judgments about freedom and responsibility depend on who you are? Personality differences in intuitions about compatibilism and incompatibilism', *Consciousness and Cognition*, 18 (2009), pp. 342–50
17 W. V. O. Quine, *The Time of My Life* (MIT Press, 1985), p. 9
18 Paul Feyerabend, *Killing Time* (University of Chicago Press, 1995), pp. 19–20
19 See Julian Baggini, 'Philosophical autobiography' *Inquiry*, vol. 45, no. 2 (2002), pp. 1–18, from which the bulk of this paragraph was drawn.
20 Tamler Sommers, *Relative Justice* (Princeton University Press, 2012), pp. 28–9
21 Mark Johnston, 'Human Beings', *Journal of Philosophy*, 84 (1987), p. 59
22 Ibid., p. 66
23 Plato, *Meno*, 80d (Hackett, 1980), p. 13
24 Eddy Nahmias, 'Intuitions about free will, determinism and by-passing' in Robert Kane (ed.), *The Oxford Handbook of Free Will* (Oxford University Press, 2011), p. 557
25 Tamler Sommers, *Relative Justice* (Princeton University Press, 2012), p. 2
26 Jennifer Veale, 'South Korea's Collective Guilt', *Time*, 18 April 2007
27 Tamler Sommers, *Relative Justice* (Princeton University Press, 2012), p. 65
28 Richard E. Nisbett, *The Geography of Thought* (Nicholas Brealey Publishing, 2005), pp. 6, 158
29 Tamler Sommers, *Relative Justice* (Princeton University Press, 2012), p. 51
30 Ibid., pp. 54–5
31 Ibid., p. 64

Chapter 9: The Waiter

1 Jean-Paul Sartre, *Being and Nothingness*, trans. Hazel Barnes (Washington Square Press, 1984), pp. 59–60
2 'Nietzsche on Free Will, Autonomy, and the Sovereign Individual', Ken Gemes in *Nietzsche on Freedom and Authority*, eds Ken Gemes and Simon May (Oxford University Press, 2009), p. 38
3 Ibid., p. 321
4 Michael Frede, *A Free Will* (University of California Press, 2011), p. 8
5 Susan Wolf, 'Asymmetrical Freedom' in Derk Pereboom (ed.), *Free Will* (Hackett, 2009), p. 237
6 See, for example, Martha Nussbaum, *Women and Human Development: The Capabilities Approach* (Cambridge University Press, 2001)
7 Tamler Sommers, *Relative Justice* (Princeton, University Press, 2012), p. 127
8 John Martin Fischer, Robert Kane, Derk Pereboom and Manuel Vargas, *Four Views on Free Will* (Blackwell, 2007), p. 82
9 Sam Harris, *Free Will* (Free Press, 2012), p. 45

Index

abuse, substance, 158
Adler, Jonathan, 148
Adshead, Gwen, 121, 124–6,
    128, 131, 137–8, 147–9
Agamemnon, 202
agency, 148–9, 206
    collective, 202
agent-causation, 19–21
Alcoholic Anonymous, 159, 174
Alexander of Aphrodisias, 130
Aliaksandrau, Andrei, 103–4,
    106–8, 110, 113–14
all-things-considered judgement,
    171–2, 177
Anderson, Philip W., 38
aporia, 182–3
Aristotle, 47, 78, 111, 128
Athill, Diana, 88
Augustine, 10, 80
autonomy, 101, 143, 151, 172–4,
    200, 212, 214

bad faith, 207
Bargh, John, 34
Barthes, Roland, 98–9

Basic Argument, 76
Baumeister, Roy, 147, 150, 160
Bayle, Pierre, 168
Beck, Friedrich, 19
behaviour modification, 136,
    146–7
Berlin, Isaiah, 105
Bernstein Center for
    Computational
    Neuroscience, 44
Berridge, Kent, 163
Blackburn, Simon, 32
Blakemore, Colin, 32
blame 119–20, 122–3, 126, 129,
    130, 134–6, 140, 145–7,
    149, 151
    affective vs detached, 149
    vs praise, 119, 130, 135–6,
        140, 145–6, 151
Borges, Jorge Luis, 215
Bouchard, Thomas, 59
Bradbury, Ray, 13, 89, 93
brain, 12, 29–33, 38, 42, 44,
    48–9, 57–8, 78, 93, 100,
    115, 134

Breen, Mike, 201
Broadmoor, 121, 124–5, 131,
    137, 147
Buridan's Ass, 112
butterfly effect, 13

Calvin, John, 80
Carnegie, Dale, 98
causal closure of the physical
    domain, 14
causal efficacy of thoughts, 33–4
caveat emptor, 214
Centers for Disease Control and
    Prevention, 151
chaos theory, 13–14
character, 75, 208
Chariots of Fire, 88
Cho, Seung-Hui, 201, 204
choice, 159, 206–10, 214–15
Churchland, Patricia, 131–4,
    138, 143–4, 189, 191
Chwast, Seth, 91
Clarke, Randolph, 198
Coleridge, Samuel Taylor, 90
Collins, Francis, 61
compulsion, 158–60, 168
compatibilism, 54, 56–7, 77,
    102, 129, 142, 153, 186,
    191–2, 194, 198
complexity theory, 39–40
control, 88–9, 91, 98, 116, 124,
    141–2
    conscious, 88–9, 91, 98, 116
    regulative vs guidance, 142
    ultimate, 141
consciousness, 2, 24, 30–1,
    36–40, 42–8, 56, 78, 89,

92, 100, 114–15, 127, 182,
    193, 199, 209
Consequence Argument, 12
constructionism, 38
'could have done otherwise',
    48–50, 52–4, 58, 72–4, 93,
    110, 119, 122, 134, 136,
    140, 142, 145, 147, 153–4,
    156, 166, 168, 174–5, 209
creativity, 89–91, 93–4, 98, 167,
    200, 211
criminal behaviour, 151
criminal justice, 4, 81, 131,
    146, 152–3, 155–6, 212

DSM-5, 158
Darwin, Charles, 2
Dawkins, Richard, 2, 120
death of the self, 98, 100
decision–making, 29, 31, 35,
    44–5, 49–51, 78, 108, 115,
    158
definition, 197–8
degrees of freedom, 5, 106,
    116, 158
deliberation, 4, 20, 24, 44,
    47–8, 91–2, 106, 109,
    114–16, 142, 150, 210
Dennett, Daniel, 77, 119, 127,
    149–50, 192–3, 195
dependence, substance, 158
Descartes, René, 37, 112
determinism, 12–15, 42, 50–51,
    54–7, 77, 82, 101–2, 111,
    115, 136, 144, 168, 183,
    199, 215
deterrence, 152–4